# Acting in
# Industrials

# Acting in Industrials

## The Business of Acting for Business

*William Paul Steele*

*Heinemann*
*Portsmouth, NH*

**Heinemann**
A division of Reed Elsevier Inc.
361 Hanover Street
Portsmouth, NH 03801–3912

*Offices and agents throughout the world*

Every effort has been made to contact the copyright holders for permission to reprint borrowed material. We regret any oversights that may have occurred and would be happy to rectify them in future printings of this work.

Figures 3.1, 3.2, 3.4, 4.1, 4.2: courtesy of John Bowman, University of Southern Maine. Figure 5.1: Janice Wayne photo by Jim Redding; Ted Norton photo by Bill Smith Studios; Linda Carole Pierce photo by Pete Dickerson; Cope Murray and Polly Cottam photos by Linda Holt. Figure 5.2: photo by Pete Dickerson. Back cover: photo by Lynn Wayne.

*Acquisitions Editor:* Lisa A. Barnett
*Production Editor:* Renée M. Pinard
*Interior Designer:* George McLean

**Library of Congress Cataloging-in-Publication Data**

Steele, William Paul.
   Acting in industrials : the business of acting for business / William Paul Steele.
      p.   cm.
   ISBN 0-435-08640-5 (alk. paper)
   1. Motion picture acting.   2. Acting for television.   3. Motion pictures in industry.   4. Industrial television.   5. Video recordings.   I. Title.
PN1995.9.A26S74   1994                          94-7635
791.43'023—dc20                                  CIP

Printed in the United States of America on acid-free paper
99   98   97   96   95   94   BB   1   2   3   4   5   6

# Contents

# Preface

This ain't Hollywood here, but don't give industrial video a bum rap.

— Bob Boyd
Independent Producer

Lights! Camera! Action! And off you go. You've been cast in your first corporate "industrial film." But it's not really a film. It's being shot on videotape for a dog food manufacturer, and you've been hired to act as an on-camera narrator to impart new product information to company employees.

There you are, all dressed up in a suit. You're standing in a warehouse facing a small camera and performing in front of a camera operator/director, a lighting/sound technician, and a handful of hard-hat-wearing folks who've taken a break from their warehousing duties to gawk at you.

It's cold in that warehouse, and it's noisy too. But you know what? You're darn glad to be there. You've spent considerable time and energy trying to crack the industrials market in your area. You've sent out dozens and dozens of headshots and resumes, taken courses in on-camera narration, corporate role playing, and auditioning. And you know that if you do a good job here you'll probably be asked back, which means that you'll be able to parlay this acting engagement into many many more.

Corporate video (which is really a more accurate description today than the time-worn "industrial film" classification) is the acting industry's rising star. It's an area that, in spite of recessionary pressures, continues to undergo sustained growth.

Corporations large and small all over the world increasingly use video and film (though film is much more expensive and less common than video) for their internal and external communications, and they use both professionals and amateurs as talent.

Maybe corporate video "ain't Hollywood." It isn't legitimate theater either. But for many actors who take corporate video seriously, it can mean the difference between a career and a part-time vocation.

If you are an aspiring actor or an actor already working professionally but not plugged into the world of industrials, you need to understand how this market works and what makes it different from the other acting markets. You need to know how to break in and how to act *in a businesslike manner* in the corporate environment. Above all, you must understand that *industrials offer the second-largest volume of work available to actors today.*

Many actors who are not in the know just don't believe the amount of work available in industrials, or at least they choose not to believe it, preferring to bury their heads in the sand and dream only of stage and screen stardom. How foolish.

Industrial video, as nuts and bolts as it may be, offers real acting opportunities for serious dramatic actors. It also offers real paychecks, paychecks that just might make it possible for those naysayers to afford more "legitimate" acting opportunities.

To illustrate my point, consider this scenario: You're single, you've just landed a professional job at a small repertory theater in a medium-sized city of about two hundred thousand people, and you're doing Williams and Miller and O'Neill. Pretty heady. Your dream come true.

The trouble is you're getting less than Actors' Equity minimum. A lot less: Saying $225 per week would be on the high side of reality. After the theater manager has taken out the required deductions, your take-home pay is around $190, which is $9,880 a year if you're lucky enough to have a fifty-two-week contract. Can you live on that?

Not if you're like most of the actors I know. So you'll need to supplement your income with what one of my actor friends calls a "job-job," or you'll have to find additional acting opportunities. And that means commercials, industrials, and print—the acting avenues that pay the bills.

Most actors I know have figured out commercials and print, but surprisingly few really understand how to succeed in industrials. And many others don't understand the scope of the field.

This book was written after *Stay Home and Star: A Step-by-Step Guide to Starting Your Regional Acting Career*[1] hit the bookstores in January of 1992. I included a substantial chapter in that book on the subject of corporate and educational markets, but after discussions with several actors and academic colleagues, I decided to widen the discussion to provide the professional and educational communities with a useful and complete guide to the growing resource of industrials. I believe that a book for actors on the inner workings of the industrial video business should have its own place on the shelf. Certainly current employment trends, if not common sense, make such a book a necessity.

And before I go further, I want to clarify what is meant by *industrials*. For the purpose of this discussion, the term is being used comprehensively to include informational videos and films made primarily by corporations but also by government agencies (including the military), educational institutions, and hospitals for noncommercial broadcast use.

Before the advent of videotape, these types of film projects were lumped by the actors' unions (the Screen Actors' Guild [SAG] and the American Federation of Television

---

1. Published by Heinemann, 361 Hanover Street, Portsmouth, NH, 03801-3912.

and Radio Artists [AFTRA]) under the "industrial film" designation and are now placed together in the "industrial/non-broadcast" designation. The word *film* is gone.

If you're skeptical about the scope of this market, consider the survey of SAG and AFTRA regional offices I conducted in January of 1993. At that time, they *all* indicated that nonbroadcast industrials were among their top income producers for both union and nonunion actors, in spite of the long recession that began in the late 1980s. And they *all* said that this market is undergoing sustained growth and *will continue to grow* for the foreseeable future. Let's look at a few illustrations.

> Cleveland. Industrials rank first in the importance of acting jobs in the Cleveland area, which includes all of Ohio, western Pennsylvania, Indiana, and West Virginia. Industrials are so important here because this is a heavy manufacturing center led by the medical and biotechnology industries. Most of the work in this region falls into the voice-over category, and a great deal is done under union contract. There is, however, plenty of nonunion work available, too.

> Denver. This region boasts an industrials market running neck and neck with commercials as the top income producer for actors, with a heavy emphasis on nonunion opportunities.

> Houston. In this region of big oil, chemical, and medical companies, it's not surprising that industrials have a strong foothold. Currently they represent 15 percent of the acting marketplace and are growing steadily. Since Texas is a right-to-work state, there are plenty of opportunities for nonunion actors.

Similar stories are told in Atlanta, Boston, Philadelphia, San Diego, Dallas, New York, St. Louis, Chicago, and many more large- and medium-sized cities. Get the picture? Industrials represent big money for actors *nationwide*.

Here's a suggestion I made in *Stay Home and Star* and re-iterate here: If you're just starting your acting career, one of the cities that is home to a SAG office is a good place to begin. Put aside your notions of New York or Hollywood.

If you pick a *regional* city where there's plenty of acting activity in commercials, industrials, print, and theater, your chances of actually working will be far greater. Why? *Much less competition and more job opportunities.* This is particularly true for the industrials category.

There's an old but often sadly true joke about the progression of an actor's career.

> *Stage One:* "Bill Steele? Who's Bill Steele?"
> *Stage Two:* "Get me Bill Steele."
> *Stage Three:* "Get me a Bill Steele type."
> *Stage Four:* "Get me a young Bill Steele."
> *Stage Five:* "Bill Steele? Who's Bill Steele?"

In the industrials arena, unlike the worlds of theatrical film and television commercials, you may just have more staying power in the "Get me Bill Steele" stage of your career.

Read *Acting in Industrials: The Business of Acting for Business* and you'll learn (hopefully) what you'll need to know to succeed in the industrials marketplace as a businessperson and not just as an actor. This book includes:

- An overview of corporate video with profiles of typical corporate video departments.
- The wide variety of subject matter and video styles used by corporations large and small.
- What is essential for you to know about corporate video production.
- Self-promotion techniques used by successful actors in the industrials field.
- Proven job search techniques.

- Preparation techniques, including understanding how to use the business actor's tools.
- How to work in the corporate environment.
- How to work alongside nonprofessional in-house talent.
- Tips on running your own acting "business," and much much more.

And when you've finished, I think you'll agree that there's more to industrials than might first meet the eye. In fact, you'll probably discover that there may be a career for you in acting for business. Industrials may not be Hollywood, but they could be much more consistent in paying the bills than Hollywood.

Certainly there are plenty of variables that go into a successful business acting career, variables such as looks, voice quality, and acting ability, to state the obvious. But having the right look or the right voice may not be enough. And great actors don't always succeed here.

*The difference between success and failure in a business environment often boils down to whether or not you know the rules of the road.* I want to help you learn the rules. If earning a living as an actor is important to you, I think you'll be glad you did.

# Acknowledgments

This text was written with the help of many people who work in the industrial film arena as actors, directors, writers, producers, and technicians. Without their assistance the comprehensive nature of this work would not have been possible. Specifically, I want to thank Bob Boyd, Bob Feldman, and Web Lithgow for their overall contributions, which included in-depth interviews on various subjects, reading draft copies, and keeping me on the right path. Thanks go as well to the following for their assistance in specialized areas: Lynn Wayne, Maggie Trichon, Cynthia Barnett, Carol Nadell, Mike Lemon, Nancy Doyle, Tersh Raybold, Don Blank, Lyle Sorensen, Ed Gillenwater, Paul Argerow, Cathy O'Toole, Larry Crowley, Connie Leaverton, Ron Baer, Michael Howard, Jim Hanna, Ann Whalen, Jerry Engleson, Doris Silk, Sylvia Gill, Linda Mackintosh, and Michael Currie.

I also want to thank Addy Harkavy for her contributions to the style of the book, the University of Southern Maine for awarding me a sabbatical leave to write it, and the John Anson Kittridge Educational Fund for travel assistance.

Finally, and most importantly, I want to thank my wife, Eleanor, for her support and editorial assistance.

# Industrial Video Overview

What's the future of corporate video? It's very bright, especially for media-based training.

— *Bob Feldman*
*Independent Producer*

Video has become the major way many corporations and businesses, educational institutions, and the government communicate with their employees and customers today. It has become a very powerful business tool.

Video can reduce the cost of training, educating, and imparting information because it is more efficient than live presentations and printing reading matter. Time is saved when a twenty- to thirty-minute video can accomplish the same training objective as a one-hour to hour-and-a-half (or longer) live course or a thirty-page manual. Almost all of the video producers and managers interviewed for this book spoke to this point, as did casting directors and agents.

Training and information delivery are more focused in video than they are in live presentations, and because

*1*

the "TV generation" is accustomed to receiving information visually, video programs have more retentive staying power.

Additionally, video programs ensure that all viewers receive the desired information in a consistent, standardized, predesigned format, removing potential "live" delivery problems such as instructor burn-out, personality conflict, omissions, and poor organization. Standardization becomes very important, for example, in training personnel in service industries, particularly national chains.

Video also does away with classroom barriers such as room arrangement, which can leave back-of-the-class members out of the loop, and audibility, which also can discriminate against back-of-the-roomers. Video treats all viewers equally. Everybody sees the same images in the same format, and all review questions are answered uniformly for all viewers with a simple rewind and replay.

Additionally, video is a great boon to people who, in a traditional classroom atmosphere, choose to sit on their hands rather than ask a clarifying question. Shyness may not be a problem for extroverted, attention-seeking actors; but for the general population, asking a question in front of a group can be traumatic. For many, asking a question is akin to public speaking, which several researchers and major publications, such as the *Wall Street Journal,* have labeled as the single activity adult Americans fear most.

It is a simple truth that many adult classroom learners will not raise their hands to ask questions for fear of appearing "stupid" or "dumb" in front of their peers. In the era of self-instructional video, however, that fear has evaporated. Video learners can now interact with their television screens, respond to questions, and review subject matter at their own pace and in complete privacy.

Video is also more interesting, particularly when dealing with technical subject matter, because it can clearly show complex procedures in demonstrations that employ lots of visual variety. Imagine how cut and dried a traditional class on computer disk drive repair might be. A live teacher would be trying to give all of the students an equal view of almost microscopic procedures.

But put those maneuvers on video using special effects such as slow motion, close-ups, magnified photography, and graphic labeling coupled with clear voice-over instruction, and you will see the power of video as a classroom alternative. In many industrial education environments video is just flat out superior because it's easier to see and hear, can precisely depict the correct execution of a repair, and can better hold the viewer's attention. In all likelihood most viewers have grown up with television as their primary supplier of information. On top of that, users can pause, rewind, and repeat important sections of the tape at will.

Additionally, video can train through the use of drama, using actors to portray characters in real-life company situations. Viewers learn by being encouraged to emulate role models.

For example, take the widely used scenario of sales personnel demonstrating the "right" and "wrong" ways to interact with customers. It's easy to see the efficiency of video in teaching salespeople (and hundreds of other job classifications as well) how to best do their jobs. Viewers watch actor surrogates perform their own everyday tasks and interact with on-screen customers who accurately resemble customers they encounter every day. This type of cognitive learning has proven to have enormous retentive effect, even after only one viewing. It's true that a picture is worth a thousand words.

Seeing a believable actor portraying someone in your role while making mistakes and then correcting those errors is a very powerful step toward improving job performance. And sometimes the only way to improve performance in a financially feasible manner is through the medium of video or film.

When you consider the rapid technological change that occurs in almost every industry today, you must realize the importance of video in spreading the word. Informational video is no longer a frill. It's an essential tool, and it's here to stay.

Bob Feldman is right: Media-based internal training is hot, particularly in the areas of sales and skills. It's where you'll find many—if not most—industrial acting opportunities today, but the scope of the market is much broader. Corporations and institutions use videos for lots of purposes.

How about the very popular internal communication of some general corporate or institutional topic, such as new sexual harassment policies? Or internal motivational attitude-conditioning videos on topics such as compliance with environmental laws or fair employee practices? These kinds of programs are produced routinely.

Add to these types of productions the huge classification of "external communications," which can include all kinds of programs such as those designed to improve an image or educate the general public. And external sales promotional programs are done all the time that fall under the industrials umbrella.

Corporate television is yet another medium in the industrials family and includes internal live broadcast (narrowcast, actually) between a central studio and many remote corporate down-link receivers.

And there are more opportunities. Many corporations and governmental institutions today have their own video news programs, produce infomercials and do special event programming to meet a variety of needs.

Are you beginning to get the idea that there is video production aplenty to meet a wide variety of corporate and institutional requirements? You should be.

So pay attention to this chapter and the next one, too. They will help you understand the actor self-marketing strategies outlined later in this book. They'll also give you guidelines on how to behave when you're cast.

These broad categories are just the tip of the iceberg because many of them become intertwined, serving several purposes and needs. In fact, most individual corporate or institutional videos fit into two or more categories. For example, a very popular type of program employs dramatic actors to portray customers and sales personnel illustrating effective sales techniques with the object of raising sales and boosting customer satisfaction. This kind of program would be training based, but it would also be highly motivational and could foster better customer relations.

Initially, corporate and institutional *video,* as opposed to the industrial promotional or documentary *film,* was born as a tool for internal communications. Several years ago business executives and institutional leaders—primarily managers of national and regional sales forces—realized that a videotape that could be mailed might be a more cost-effective means of delivering information than would holding regular meetings and incurring high travel expenses. This simple idea, of course, has ballooned in recent years to the point where today no self-respecting large corporation or institution—even a relatively small business—can survive without video.

In many large companies and institutions, each department has its own need to generate programs, resulting in volumes of videos every year. For example, consider the largest institution of all: the United States government. I don't know how many videos are produced for government agencies, but the number must be staggering. And this means a lot of work for actors.

The large number of opportunities shouldn't be surprising. Americans have become increasingly dependent on television as their primary source of news and information and entertainment. The average American watches four to six hours of television each day, which leaves precious little time for reading.

Let's face it. Television *has* left reading in the dust as a communications tool. In fact, many employed Americans can't read *at all*. Is it any wonder that corporate television, particularly in the form of videos, is on the rise?

## ✳ *The Levels of Corporate Television Production*

To give you a better understanding of the ways in which companies and institutions use video and where actors and narrators fit into the communications arena, let us consider video production on a "levels" basis, an approach to understanding corporate television production developed by Bob Feldman of Continuum Training Corporation.

Level 1 is characterized by relatively low-quality video images that are really nothing more than glorified home movies. These productions involve little content or production preparation. They are usually in-house—which simply means company or institutional employees do the work rather than outside vendors—video recordings of live presentations. The recordings are made for posterity or because people who need the information could not attend the events. These types of video productions are called "event capture" and rarely require professional—even voice—talent.

Level 2 is distinguished by improved video images and the presence of professional talent, particularly voice talent or on-camera narrators, who are also called *spokespersons* or *spokes* in the acting business. Producers use the term *actor* when referring to people cast in dramatic situations, often called *role-plays,* which are produced at higher levels.

Budgets are necessarily low at this level. The videos are of acceptable technical quality but often lack the required up-front planning to achieve motivational value. Typical programs include such topics as technical training, where field service personnel have a procedure explained, or where hospital personnel are shown how to turn on, calibrate, and use a medical instrument. Many of these programs are lengthy. For narrators, this means lots of copy.

Level 2 production is usually highly informational and instructional rather than motivational and does not require a huge budget. For these reasons, level 2 is where the vast majority of industrials are done.

As you can see, the volume of work available to narrators in level 2 is important to consider. Because of its informational nature, an authoritative voice is usually required either on- or off-camera. Success at this level requires excellent narrative skills.

For level 2 voice-over work, a pleasing and authoritative voice and an easy-to-listen-to delivery style are paramount. On-camera narrators must also look the part and present themselves in a relaxed, natural manner. To be considered "efficient," both on- and off-camera narrators must be able to read long sections of copy without flubbing. *Efficiency* is a critically important descriptive term we'll discuss in depth later on.

Level 3 is characterized by professional-quality video images and good lighting and audio. Programs at this level are rich in both informational and motivational content. Serious content development and graphics preparation are evident in the quality of the presentation, preparation of the set or natural environment, and in all other elements of the program, particularly talent. Visual interest and attention are increased by the use of multiple places and faces. A level 3 video program may mix classroom-style presentations, interviews, straight voice-over narration, on-camera narration, customer site visits, role playing, and multiple settings. Level 3 efforts are usually targeted to professional sales, support, and marketing audiences and are intended to achieve a business or policy goal.

A good example of a level 3 program that both educates and motivates would be a typical in-house marketing presentation produced to sell a new line of equipment to a company's field distribution network. The tape might say, "Here's our new software package. Look at this demo. See how much more powerful it is than the last one." This type of video is used routinely to get field personnel behind new products or services. Such an objective can be reached in a variety of ways, but programs have to be of relatively high production quality to be taken seriously because typical viewers have a high level of built-in video savvy, *which means professional talent is necessary.*

Therefore, level 3 is where dramatic actors and on- and off-camera narrators will find the majority of their work.

Level 4 is characterized by the highest degree of production value and expertise. It's where the most money is spent and where industrials are made for the general public and for top-of-the-line in-house purposes. Typical uses include programs for resale, trade show pieces, infomercials, point-of-purchase videos, corporate overviews, government policy overviews, and the like. The object may be to motivate and entertain while educating or to serve clear public relations or sales purposes.

For example, let's say an emerging growth company finds it necessary to improve its image on Wall Street. A documentary-style, feel-good video or film designed to impress financial analysts about the growth of the business might be just the ticket.

But those analysts won't be impressed with anything but top-level production. Why not? Because they associate quality public relations with a quality product.

Therefore, level 4 productions invariably require professional talent and frequently feature a blend of dramatic scenes using on-camera narrators for introductions and transitions.

It is critical, however, that you understand that level 4 production is *not* where you will find the most acting opportunities. In terms of volume, and for reasons pegged primarily to budget, level 4 production falls way behind levels 2 and 3.

When it comes to self-marketing, to which an entire chapter is devoted later, *your efforts should aim primarily at levels 2 and 3*. You'll probably need casting agencies, independent casting directors, and perhaps even talent agents to crack level 4.

## ✳ *Profiles of Corporate Television Departments and Production Companies*

The next step in understanding the world of industrials is to take a look at the structure of corporations' internal video services departments and the independent production companies they contract with for services.

There have been many changes in the structure of corporate television departments in recent years. If you have followed publications such as *Inc. Magazine,* the *Wall Street Journal,* and *Investor's Business Daily,* you have read that corporations have been downsizing by laying people off and by cutting operating budgets severely.

So does it stand to reason that these companies' general reductions have had a negative impact on their internal video production operations? It most certainly does. Large, fast-growing internal video services departments are no longer the rule. While there are many huge corporate television operations still in evidence throughout the country, many companies have reduced their staffs and/or decided that it is far less expensive to put their video and film production projects out to competitive bid. Most governmental agencies, as well as many educational institutions, do.

Being aware of this trend alone is *vitally* important to the actor or spokesperson because it will dramatically affect self-marketing strategies. Instead of selling yourself to several autonomous departments—such as training, marketing, and public relations—you may now find yourself dealing with one internal entity that handles everything and that may even service the needs of outside clients. Or you might find that the folks at XYZ Corporation aren't there any more, and that all television work for the company is being generated by freelance writers, producers, directors, and video production and post-production houses.

But all of this downsizing and change is no great cause for alarm; as of the early and mid-nineties, there *is* growth in the overall world of industrials, albeit not the robust growth as in the early eighties.

With these thoughts in mind, let's take a look at a few examples of internal corporate and independent production setups I've divided by size.

## Large, Internal Corporate Video Departments

Consolidation has come with corporate downsizing. Significant cost savings have resulted in putting all corporate television production under one administrative roof, which makes looking for a job easier for self-marketing actors for obvious reasons. Three examples of this type of department are GTE VisNet, Georgia Pacific Television, and John Hancock Life Insurance.

In 1989 GTE Corporation, headquartered in Stamford, Connecticut, consolidated thirteen separate video production centers into a single organization called GTE VisNet, which is now made up of four major production centers located in Stamford; Thousand Oaks, California; Irving, Texas (a suburb of Dallas); and Tampa, Florida.[1] Each is a full-blown production center with its own studio.

All of the centers have four or five on-staff producer/directors and they contract the services of independent producers. VisNet also has remote, one-person operations in Durham, North Carolina; Westfield, Indiana; Atlanta, Georgia; and Honolulu, Hawaii.

Collectively, GTE VisNet is one of the largest corporate communications networks in the country and produces videos for in-house as well as outside clients. Employing both union (SAG and AFTRA) and nonunion talent, they use professional performers 85 to 90 percent of the time. Voice-over talent is almost exclusively professional.

Employment trends depend on location, which is typical of the entire industry. Outside of New York City, in Stamford, and in California, the work is almost exclusively union; but in Dallas it's a different matter. Production companies in Dallas use a mixture of union and nonunion professionals.

The Dallas SAG office reports a strong corporate video market. GTE VisNet, a major player in the Dallas industrial video arena, does produce an occasional regional commercial but concentrates on business television. At this writing GTE VisNet is working with internal executives to make them comfortable on camera working alongside professional talent for spontaneous live broadcasts on the corporation's extensive satellite network. GTE has more than four hundred down-links across the country and is convinced that live broadcast that features more and more company employees is the wave of the future.

---

1. Information on the structure of GTE VisNet provided by Ed Gillenwater, Manager of Media Development and Production, GTE VisNet, Irving, Texas.

But the use of internal workers does not spell doom for actors or narrators. Satellite broadcast is, in truth, just another opportunity. Actors and narrators are being integrated into the roles of program hosts, talk-show hosts, and moderators for panels for live broadcast.

In addition, actors and narrators are being hired with increasing frequency for interactive television projects, which GTE reports is a fast-growing area of production.

Georgia Pacific Television (GPT) in Atlanta, Georgia, is a wholly owned profit center that markets itself, like GTE Vis-Net, to in-house as well as outside clients.[2]

GPT is extremely busy, producing over two hundred programs per year using union or nonunion voice-over or on-camera narrators *in every production*. Thirty to 40 percent of these productions employ role-playing actors as well. Relying on two complete studios, mobile trucks, and field units, GPT produces a blend of in-house and outside corporate videos, television commercials, live broadcast, and teleconferencing sessions. Obviously GTP is a place to get to know if you're in Atlanta.

Four in-house producers handle about 120 shows, while the rest—the smaller productions—are controlled by directors who also run camera.

John Hancock's single television studio is located at company headquarters in Boston, Massachusetts, where their Video Communications Department produces forty to sixty tapes a year for in-house use with a staff of thirteen people, six or seven of whom are producers.[3]

John Hancock uses professional talent, primarily voice talent, for most tapes. In recent years the company has reduced the number of on-camera narrators hired and only oc-

---

2. Information on Georgia Pacific Television provided by Don Blank, director of television production, Georgia Pacific Corporation.
3. Information on John Hancock Life Insurance video communications provided by Lyle Sorensen, video producer.

casionally uses actors in role-plays. John Hancock mostly books union members.

## Medium and Small Departments

The vast majority of in-house corporate video departments fall into the medium or small categories. Let's take a look at one of each, Key Corporation and Bath Iron Works, which were chosen as illustrations because their setups are widely duplicated.

Key Corp's Corporate Audio-Visual Services is a two-man shop servicing just under nine hundred Key Bank branch offices nationwide.[4] Unlike its larger counterparts, Key Corp has no studio, employs outside vendors, and rents outside studios and equipment when needed. The Audio-Visual Services department has two locations—Portland, Maine, and Albany, New York—where approximately twenty-five videos are produced each year. Each of those locations is equipped with offices, a complete editing suite, and field units.

Key Corp hires professional talent for roughly three-quarters of their productions, mostly voice-overs. They do employ a few on-camera narrators each year, produce a regular news program using professionals, and occasionally use actors for role-plays. Key Corp hires primarily nonunion talent found through casting agencies.

Bath Iron Works in Bath, Maine, is typical of one-person shops that do everything for a company from image pieces to hard-core industrial safety training. This famous shipbuilding company cranks out several tapes a year through its video production department, using professional voice-over and on-camera narrators, both union and nonunion.

---

4. Information on Key Corp Corporate Audio-Visual Services provided by Paul Argerow, manager.

## Independent Production Houses

Large or small, independent video production houses all serve the same general function when it comes to corporations and institutions: They aid in the production of videos and films. Many of them produce television commercials as well.

The D. I. Group of Boston, Massachusetts, is a large independent production house that has a staff of over fifty people, including four producers and one creative director.[5] This company produces many different types of films and videos, including over one hundred in the corporate category each year. They also hire freelance producers and directors.

D. I. has two studios and a dining facility and is a signatory to the current SAG and AFTRA contracts, which means they employ *only* union actors, narrators, and spokespersons.

Gilmore Associates of Boston, Massachusetts, is a medium to small production facility that has a staff of approximately ten people: a producer, director, two editors, several salespeople, and a manager.[6] Gilmore produces fifteen to twenty corporate videos yearly, including projects for the largest "corporation" in the world, the United States government.

When things get busy, Gilmore hires freelancers for a variety of positions and uses professional talent for most projects, including role-playing actors and both on- and off-camera narrators. Gilmore hires both union and nonunion talent.

Walkabout Productions of Austin, Texas, is a sole proprietor production company that creates videotapes for industry between five and thirty times a year, depending on

---

5. Information on the D. I. Group provided by Cathy O'Toole, manager.

6. Information on Gilmore Associates provided by Larry Crowley, company manager.

the year.[7] Operating out of her home in Austin, Connie Leaverton hires freelancers for all her jobs, rents studios and equipment, and uses professional talent as role-players and on- and off-camera narrators, both union and nonunion.

Walkabout represents the small level of production companies and is followed in size only by independent producers and directors who hire themselves out as freelancers to all levels of production houses and corporations.

Due to economic realities and the resulting corporate downsizing of internal video service departments, there has been a wide proliferation of independent producers and directors, many of whom work as freelancers for the very corporations who used to employ them full time. These people will be particularly important to remember when I discuss self-promotion.

Now you have a general overview of corporate video production. Next let's examine what you can do to prepare yourself for *working* in industrials.

---

7. Information on Walkabout provided by Connie Leaverton, owner.

# Making the Business Transition

Bill, you're too big for us.

— *Web Lithgow*
*Director, Commonwealth Films*

**W**hen Web Lithgow discreetly drew me aside during an industrial shoot for a video called "The Deposition" and made the above observation, he didn't have to say any more. I knew right then and there what the trouble was.

He was referring to the histrionic, overly theatrical approach I was taking to my character, who was a young executive learning the ropes of answering questions under oath during a deposition. Even though this event occurred fairly early in my business acting career, I was nonetheless a veteran and should have known better. I had forgotten for a moment the difference between stage and screen technique.

## ✳ Stage vs. Film Acting Technique

Acting is acting, right? Everybody wants to see believable characterizations whether it's on a stage or on a screen. And to be believable the actor must be truthful, whatever the medium.

But the approach taken to arrive at that honest performance depends on the nature of the audience. To put it simply, stage actors have to play to a theater full of people. Screen actors, on the other hand, have to play to just one person, represented by a camera in a studio. *It's a question of distance.*

The degree to which stage actors have to play to a theater full of people varies. If those people are within a few feet of the actors as in small auditoriums or theaters-in-the-round, a technique akin to film acting may be required. But if the theater is large and the audience spread out, it is incumbent upon the actor to communicate fully with the people who are farthest away. Stage actors know this.

Gestures, expressions, and movement are often larger than life in live theater, so they may be seen by all. The problem is they are frequently perceived as *indicated* by the folks down front who are deprived of naturalistic subtlety.

When an actor "indicates" a reaction or feeling with something contrived, such as a too-large gesture or an overdone facial expression, the audience that is aware of the contrivance may have to work harder to suspend their disbelief. For them, the world of the play is changed to the world of the indicating actor. Moral: Avoid sitting in the front rows of a large theatrical auditorium.

If you accept the idea that all *screen* actors play *only* to the people down front, then you must also accept the fact that indicated behavior will ring untrue to your *entire* audience. For the screen actor, *less is more.* This is particularly true for the business actor, who must often act as a role model.

As Web Lithgow told me, "The less you do the more believable you are, and the baseline of working in front of the camera is believability. If you're not believable, you've got *nothing.*"

Everything you do in front of the camera must be completely truthful in terms of the character you are playing. Your characterization has to be real for you if you expect it to be real for the audience, even if the character you play is yourself in a spokesperson role. And on camera that means playing it small, as small as real life. Even smaller if you're in a close-up. Remember that a clear thought on camera is enough. On stage that thought must be externalized.

## Read Books, Take Classes

Perhaps the most important first step you can take to prepare yourself for the transition to acting in industrials is to read some *good* books on acting, of which there are many. And then take acting lessons. If you've done all that and feel you already know how to act, take a good *film* acting course or two and experience the difference in technique. Learn how to keep everything small and do everything simply. And most importantly, look at your on-camera work and consider constructive critiques carefully.

I've emphasized the word *good* above because there are plenty of bad acting texts out there and lots of bad acting classes and teachers. One way to ensure you'll have positive educational experiences is to network with successful actors in your area. Check with the SAG or Actors' Equity Association local office, if there's one near you, for recommendations. Explore nearby college and university offerings. Take the initiative to find out what's good in your area and then participate.

Years ago when industrial films were relatively unsophisticated, many actors learned their on-screen craft on the job. But those days are history. *If you can't demonstrate that you understand the requirements of the camera come audition time, you'll never get on the job.*

## Actors vs. On-Camera Narrators

The second step in your transition is to clearly understand one of the most misunderstood realities of the acting business: the difference between *role-playing actors* and *on-camera narrators* or *spokespersons.*

You already learned in chapter 1 that producers routinely use the term *actor* when referring to people cast in dramatic situations, and *narrator* or *spokesperson* when referring to people cast as on-camera imparters of information or hosts. *Narrator* is a term also used to identify people who are hired as voice-over artists who read informative, educational, or documentary-style scripts.

For some unknown reason, most producers think that playing "yourself" as a spokesperson or narrator is different from playing the role of someone else. But fundamentally it's not. Not when you're reaching for honesty.

Truth is truth. The "self" you play must be as believable as the "character" you play. And the road to believability is the same in either case. Therefore narrators must turn their narrations into stream-of-consciousness monologues. So for the rest of this book I'm going to refer to all performers, even narrators, as actors.

Remember that about 70 percent of the roles cast in industrials today are narrative roles, so if you want to really score in this business you'd better learn how to play yourself with complete honesty.

So add to your acting curriculum a course or two in on-camera narration and voice-over narration to get used to the idea that narrating is acting, too. You have to believe in what you're reading if you expect others to believe in you.

## ✳ Developing an Executive Point of View

Think ahead for a moment and imagine the kinds of people you'll be exposed to in the world of industrials. Who are they? What are they like?

Of course you're going to meet in-house creative people such as writers, directors, and producers. You'll also work with technical personnel such as camera operators, video editors, set and lighting directors, and floor managers. But you will also be exposed to an entirely different layer of corporate employees: executives and institutional leaders. And these folks are among the most important to you.

Executives in the form of managers, vice presidents, presidents, agency heads, and CEOs are the *clients* of the creative cadre. They commission the videos and films in which you hope to star. And what is the one thing most successful executives have in common? Their conservative style.

Web Lithgow, who's worked with executives around the country, says,

> In most industries and government agencies there is a uniform for the office professional: suit, shirt, and tie. Trim haircut. Little facial hair. Serious glasses. And a uniform code of behavior. There are exceptions. Engineers—Silicon Valley execs, for example—dress down and act casual. East Coast execs are more buttoned up, as are all bigger city execs.

The executive breed in general really does like to play it middle of the road in almost everything. They're cautious about what they say and wear; they try to project an air of confidence at all times. For example, let's look at a typical insurance company.

One I know well is the UNUM Corporation, in Portland, Maine. Over the years I've performed in several of their videos, which were shot on location in various offices and conference rooms at corporate headquarters. And you know what? In all my years of working at UNUM I have never seen an executive wearing anything but basic business attire. Men and women all wear suits.

This does not mean, however, that these people are *formal*. They're not. You'll see plenty of people in shirtsleeves at UNUM. But ties stay on. And women's blouses are all business.

And the conversation is not formal, but it is reserved. Call it reserved informality. Polite and considered. You won't see UNUM executives getting all gushy about anything. Like good card players they play the daily game close to the vest. And so do all the executives I've observed in all the corporations I've worked for nationwide.

These executives are vitally important to you because they exert great influence on video production.

## ❋ Genesis of a Video

Here's a typical scenario. Jim, a vice president of microwave oven sales for a national appliance corporation, needs a video to give his sales force an edge in selling ovens to a national department store chain. Using a spokesperson, the video will extol the product's reliability and the corporation's quality service. Jim doesn't have the budget to hire a cast of several actors.

The first thing Jim will do is meet with Bob, the manager of his company's video services department, to spell out what he wants. Bob then gets a script writer to write a script and schedules studio time and personnel for an eventual shoot.

When the script is completed, it is submitted to Jim for approval. Once he gives the go-ahead a set will be designed and casting will take place. Jim will have final approval of these elements of production as well.

For *you*, this means that Jim will be the person who decides whether or not you will be cast. Not Bob. No, you probably won't meet Jim during the casting process. You probably won't meet Bob either. You'll most likely audition for the producer/director at a casting agency or be considered through your own self-marketing efforts; but the client—that's Jim—will make the final decision. And Jim won't hire anyone as a spokesperson who isn't like himself.

So your job, if you want to be cast, is to present yourself as a person he will feel comfortable with. But who is that person? Businesspeople, for the most part, are all business. They think about getting the job done, working as a team, and meeting objectives with logic, control, and competence. This is the role you must play to gain Jim's confidence.

So the next step in your transition to business actor is to develop a businesslike image and point of view. Your entire approach to this sector of the acting business must be businesslike. Your wardrobe, grooming, self-marketing tools, and even your general knowledge must all reflect this image so that the personal message you project to the business community will be perceived as trustworthy. You want to look and sound like one of them or you won't be believable or even recognizable.

Maybe this isn't what you had in mind when you decided to be a professional actor. You're a performing artist, after all, and want to be free to be as quirky and unconventional as you like. But remember Bob Boyd's warning: "This ain't Hollywood." This is business. *So if the idea of developing a businesslike image is anathema to you, think of it as just another role.*

You, the outgoing, confident businessperson who just happens to be an actor will get corporate jobs. But you, the weird and wild bohemian who is an *artiste* will get that quick (and terminal) "Thank you very much."

## Wardrobe and Make-Up

The first place to start refining your image is in the way you look. Whenever men go on an industrial audition or personal interview, they should wear a well-cut conservative suit and tie. Women should choose a suit and blouse with understated jewelry, which is particularly important when choosing earrings. No dangling earrings! Earrings must sit *on* the ear lobe. Everyone should wear well-polished shoes. You can't lose if you go with banker's gray or blue for the suit; that's what *they* wear!

Generally speaking you want to stay away from white, red, busy prints, plaids, stripes, and blacks because these colors and patterns do not translate well on television. Vertical stripes on collars—even fine, conservative ones—and in plaids make the vertical scan lines on a television screen vibrate or form patterns called *moire.*

Avoid anything flashy. Your clothes shouldn't stand out; they should blend in with what's expected. You want to look like a person who knows what she or he is talking about, and clothes that are too striking can undercut you.

Since business actors almost always provide their own wardrobes, the actor's clothes rack is being auditioned along with the actor.

In the corporate world, make-up should always be understated. Women should wear just enough to enhance their natural skin tones, and men shouldn't wear any at all. Remember that you don't want make-up to draw attention to itself in an unexpected way. Anything garish will work against you.

You will of course be carefully checked out from tip to

toe and stem to stern; make certain that all the personal messages you send out will be positively received.

## Business Accessories

My advice above also applies to the things you lug around with you, such as briefcases, portfolios, make-up kits, garment bags, and tie caddies. Everything you choose should be selected with care.

Most business actors I know show up at auditions with a book bag that houses everything they own—from a wardrobe change to cab fare—slung over their shoulders. But if you're going on an interview on corporate turf, you better look like someone who works there. Carry your headshots, resumes, and your appointment book in a brown or black leather briefcase or portfolio; when you show up on the job carry your wardrobe in something that looks like you respect your belongings. This will be noticed. We'll examine the details of headshots and resumes in a separate chapter.

If you're a regional actor seeking employment opportunities over a wide geographic area, then perhaps your largest and most expensive accessory will be an automobile. Again, choose with care.

If you're working in or around Detroit, an American-made vehicle makes obvious good sense. Maybe it makes good sense anywhere these days. Whatever you drive should blend in with your businesslike image and should be well groomed.

Finally, you should have an answering machine or service and may want to consider a car phone and/or pager. These tools will help you keep in touch and will enhance your image of professionalism.

If you decide to get an answering machine, record a simple, businesslike message such as "You've reached 123–4567. Leave a message at the beep and I'll return your call as soon as possible. Thanks." This is no place to do your Steve Martin impersonation.

## ✳ Learning About Business

Now that you're thinking and looking businesslike it's time for some education. You need to learn something about business in general.

"Oh, come on," you're thinking. "Enough is enough, already. What do I possibly need to know about business? Please, don't waste my time."

I hear this kind of comment from my industrial acting students all the time. They just want to act, not *prepare* to act. They think they can do almost anything off the top of their heads. And after I show them a few representative industrial scripts they think that any moron can be a corporate actor. Not so!

So pay attention, reader! No wiggling, no talking. I'm going to give you a very important assignment, one that will fill your head with what you need to know to get a leg up on the corporate acting competition.

Read the *Wall Street Journal, Investors Business Daily, Inc. Magazine, Fortune,* the *New York Times,* the *Washington Post,* and any other of the better business publications available almost everywhere. Read some or all of these regularly to learn about current business trends, hot new products, and important legislation affecting business to help you become knowledgeable and conversant on subjects near and dear to the hearts of the people you hope will be your future employers.

Perhaps even more importantly, you'll become familiar with the language of business, so you'll be better at interpreting those seemingly abstruse corporate scripts. Some actors I know even go so far as to read countless annual reports, mostly of Fortune 500 companies, to learn about new technology.

This kind of research will really pay off in auditions where your obvious understanding of what you're reading will lead to instant interest in *you.*

## Your Personal Demeanor

Confidence, reader, confidence. You, the well-read, well-dressed businessperson (who just happens to be an actor) must exude confidence without overkill. In every situation, audition, interview, rehearsal, and on the job, your personal demeanor should be warm but businesslike, friendly but reserved, approachable but not self-centered.

You know that famous commercial line for a popular deodorant, don't you? It goes like this: *You never get a second chance to make a good first impression.* It's true. Make your first impression a confident, businesslike one every time.

## ✳ *Practice by Reading Aloud*

How do you get to Carnegie Hall? Practice, practice, practice. In *Stay Home and Star* I urged aspiring actors to practice reading aloud. It's probably the single most important preparatory activity in which you can engage. And it has several important benefits for you in the industrial acting marketplace.

Your ability to read smoothly and without unnecessary hesitation, to use vocal variety, to develop eye contact with the camera while reading, to have the control to manipulate tempo, and to vary energy levels will be essential for both auditions and work.

I recommend that you set aside at least *fifteen minutes* every day to read aloud in the privacy of your home, using the business reading matter recommended above. This will kill two birds with one stone. Not only will you practice the technical skill of reading aloud, you'll also catch up on what's current in the business world.

Reading *smoothly and without hesitation* is a skill you'll use every time you audition for narrative roles. In an audition situation, your practice sessions will give you the confidence you need to read well under pressure. On the job, this ability will result in fewer takes and will enhance your reputation as an efficient performer.

As you begin to develop your technical reading skills, start increasing *eye contact*. When you hit the audition circuit you'll want to be able to look directly into the lens of the camera as much as possible without making mistakes. Use an inanimate object to represent a camera for this purpose. Anything will do, even a plant or spot on the wall. Scan each sentence as you read and try to look at the "camera" about halfway through. When looking at the inanimate object becomes easy, try practicing in front of a mirror so you can see how you look and how you alter your body movements to fit the material. You want to look as confident as you sound, and you need to practice subtle gestures and facial expressions. Remember the principal of distance discussed earlier.

When you're comfortable with your ability to read and make eye contact, add practice sessions where you concentrate on *vocal variety* such as rate (speed), volume and pitch, emphasizing key words, and *energy*. Your ability to alter these elements smoothly will aid you greatly when it comes time to take direction.

## ✳ Memorization

Finally, you'll need to practice *memorization* so that you can accomplish this chore as efficiently as possible. Even with such technological advances as teleprompters and earprompters, the call for memorization is still great, particularly in dramatic situations. Most directors prefer not to use prompters of any kind for dramatic pieces, rightly believing that a memorized performance will be better—stronger, more natural, and more convincing.

In a survey of directors and producers undertaken for this book, very few respondents indicated a partiality to prompters in dramatic situations. In fact, all respondents indicated that, in their opinion, prompters have a negative impact on spontaneity in dramatic scenes. While this impression can be vigorously debated by prompter advocates, the reality of the situation demands that actors who want to work in dramatic industrial presentations be prepared to memorize. Fortunately, on-camera narrators are now almost universally allowed to use prompting devices, which will be discussed fully later.

Memorization techniques I will leave up to you. Most actors I know hate the process and have arrived, by trial and error, at an efficient method.

Good dramatic film actors will tell you that they never learn the text of a script so cold that they're locked into it instead of the stimuli that makes the text happen. They reason that if you're tied to words instead of the ideas behind them, you're asking for trouble. But corporate actors, in most situations, have to be *very* true to the script, exactly as written.

Consider what Don Blank of Georgia Pacific Television has to say about memorization.

> Corporate actors have a memorization problem to a degree because industrials do not allow a lot of latitude. You pretty much have to deliver the script exactly the way it's written. You can't ad lib your way through a scene or develop a scene the way you sometimes can in a dramatic feature. In corporate video you have to develop the character and make sure you're saying all the relevant buzzwords correctly. . . . You also have long blocks of copy to deal with.

These observations speak for themselves. The savvy business actor knows how to memorize lots of copy relatively quickly. It's an essential skill.

If you don't know how to start, try memorizing this section of this chapter using the line-by-line method. Start with sentence one, repeating it over and over aloud until you feel ready to add sentence two.

But be careful—a trap awaits. On-the-set changes such as copy changes or alterations in interpretation requested by the director are common. If you've memorized too well, you may have lost flexibility. Therefore, don't learn the words cold. Be able to accommodate requests for change. Try practicing rememorizing.

## ✳ The Union Debate

Certainly an important consideration in preparing yourself for the industrial market is whether or not to join AFTRA, SAG, or both. Depending upon where you live, it may be a difficult choice.

If you are a major-market actor who lives in a union town and are a person who wants to work in *all* areas of the business, membership in the unions will be a must. But small-city actors who want to specialize in industrials may want to go nonunion.

Consider this: *All* of the SAG and AFTRA representatives interviewed for this book lamented the fact that there is plenty of nonunion industrial work available to actors in their regions. They also indicated casting agencies routinely hold auditions for nonunion jobs. Message? A union card is not a necessity for success as a business actor, but it may be for success as a comprehensive actor. The choice is entirely up to you and depends on how you want to pursue your individual acting career.

You should be aware that many corporations, institutions, and production houses *prefer* to use nonunion talent to reduce costs and paperwork. You should also know that joining a union means that you will no longer be permitted to perform in industrials unless they fall under union jurisdiction.

Both unions have the same general rules. Members may not agree to work for any producer who is not a signatory—meaning they have signed an agreement to abide by union rules of employment—unless the booking is handled through a paymaster who is a signatory. The paymaster is then the employer of record and must assure that the production abides by union work rules and rates.

It is the member's responsibility to contact the unions to verify a producer's signatory status before accepting a job offer. Members may not work for any producer against whom the union is conducting a strike or violate any strike order of the union. And it is a member's responsibility to report a violation of union rules to the union.

The union takes these rules very seriously. Members who are brought up on charges of violating union rules face fines, sanctions, and public confessions before the membership. If you aren't ready to abide by the rules, you shouldn't join.

The information in this book applies to acting in industrials whether or not you belong to a union. If you are not yet a member and wonder whether or not to join, you should carefully investigate the employment opportunities in the area in which you work or would like to work before you decide. Ask around. Check with both union and nonunion actors in your area and with producers and casting directors.[1]

---

1. In *Stay Home and Star,* I wrote a section on whether or not to join the actors' unions and how to gain membership. See pages 6 through 8 and Appendix A in that volume if you have further questions regarding the unions.

# Video Production Essentials for Actors

Lots of actors, when they're starting out, aren't even aware of how their behavior impacts on editing. They need to know more about production.

— *Ron Baer*
*Norwest Productions*

*T*o avoid problems and be as successful as you want to be, there are certain elements of on-camera and audio-booth television production that you should be familiar with before you go on the job.

For on-camera actors, these elements include your relationship with the camera and the microphone, your understanding of timing and movement as it applies to post-production, and your relationship with production personnel. Your proficiency with studio and personal prompting devices will be discussed separately.

Voice-over performers need to know who's who in audio production and how to work the microphone through alterations in pitch, inflection, rate, volume, and timing.

Understand that the following discussion cannot replace a good general text or two on television production and taking comprehensive film acting and voice courses. But what is discussed here may save you much heartache and help you work in a professional manner when the lights are on for real.

## ✳ Who's Who in Production

No professional actor should ever show up on an industrial shoot without knowing the roles of the many people he or she will encounter. This kind of knowledge promotes teamwork, a necessary ingredient in successful programming. Here is a brief glossary of production personnel:

- The *producer* is responsible for the entire production, including the coordination of all of its elements, from casting to editing. In the corporate television arena, the producer is often the writer and director as well.

- The *associate producer* acts as an assistant to the producer by coordinating production necessities, such as prop procurement, arranging schedules, booking hotels, and talent payment. This person handles the day-to-day busywork every production requires, allowing the producer to concentrate more closely on production quality.

- The *director* is charged with directing on-camera talent and all technical personnel during the shoot to transform the written script into an effective video or film, including all audio portions.

- The *production assistant* aids the producer and director during the creative process of shooting by keeping an eye on continuity and by performing a myriad of other functions, including writing notes regarding good and bad takes. This person is also a communication link between actors and director.

- The *floor manager* is responsible for all studio activities in live and live-on-tape programs. This person relays director cues and comments to actors on the "floor" (while the director is in the studio making shot selection decisions), and supervises all floorpersons through the technical director.

- *Floorpersons* is a generic term used to identify the various categories of grip or stagehand you are likely to meet, including cue card holders, teleprompter operators, boom microphone operators, camera dollie operators, camera cable pullers, prop adjustors, lighting personnel, set dressers, and prop people.

- The *technical director* is responsible for setting and lighting design and also may be on hand to direct scenic touch-ups and the lighting of talent. Most of the grips are under this person's direct command. On some shoots this category will be referred to as the *lighting designer* or *gaffer.*

- *Camera operators* operate the camera at the pleasure of the director. Sometimes, on high-end productions (usually film), the camera operator is called the *director of photography.*

- The *audio engineer* is in charge of all audio elements of the shoot and is someone with whom actors must develop a strong working relationship. In large studio productions, the audio engineer may be based in the control room operating an audio board mixing the sound coming from several microphones. In such cases there will be an audio assistant who works with the actors. Audio engineers often work in the studio holding boom microphones.

These are the people you're most likely to work with in industrials. But you should know that on most shoots you'll probably run into only a few of these folks, even in a studio environment. On remote shoots—shoots shot on location—production personnel are often kept to a bare minimum. On industrial on-location shoots—in corporate offices and the like—remember that all the other people you see at desks and in the hallways *work there,* and you will be expected to respect their business environment.

Often the producer and director are a single individual, and the camera operator will set the talent lighting and be assisted by one grip who will perform many additional tasks. It is only in the very largest and highest budget shoots that you run into a production army.

## ✳ *On-Camera Considerations*

### The Camera as a Person

Even though the majority of industrials are shot more simply than features, you still are working in front of a camera or two and you need to know what to expect and what's expected of you.

Television is with good reason often referred to as "the close-up medium." The camera, unlike the eye of the live viewer, observes you in *minute* detail and is totally unforgiving, particularly in close-up. Every movement and nuance of your behavior, however slight, is magnified by the camera and intimately revealed to the screen where the viewer does not feel it necessary to politely turn away when you do something personal. When the camera is on you, there is nowhere to hide when you scratch a blemish or unconsciously change a facial expression to reveal that you are nervous or that you have forgotten what to say or where to move.

This means that when you are in front of the camera you must carefully control everything you do. Remember, this is not a stage performance, but something far more intimate and often understated. Think of it as developing a *relationship* with the lens.

## Your Relationship with the Lens

If you've been hired to perform in a dramatic situation, you will no doubt be instructed to never look into the camera. Your relationship with the lens will be someone else's responsibility. But in the bulk of industrial production, the lens will be the audience, the "person" to whom you speak. This is always true when you are an on-camera narrator or spokesperson, and it is frequently the case when you act as an interviewer, host, news anchor, or moderator.

In these "talk to the camera" situations eye contact becomes of paramount importance. You must make eye contact with the lens *as though it were a person rather than an inanimate object*. Do you know the old saying, look for the lie in the eyes? It is quite true in television.

If your eye contact is not genuine, a close-up will expose the lie. You must really *look* at the lens, not stare at it with glassy eyes. You must really *see* a person in the lens and really *believe* in the camera as an audience if you want to convince the viewer. On top of that, you must look at the lens even more than you would look in the eye of a single person.

When you communicate one-on-one with another person, too much eye contact can be perceived as threatening or as an invasion of personal space. Most people find it uncomfortable to be stared at in this way. But in television, where your viewer watches a screen, interpersonal communication manners change.

The television viewer *expects* you to maintain eye contact and psychologically considers your looking away, unless it is achieved in a completely relaxed manner and for a very short period of time, distracting because it *deintensifies* the communication process.

In your practice sessions, you need to train yourself to make as much relaxed and believable eye contact with the camera lens as possible, whether you are working from memory or with the aid of prompting devices. What works best is an occasional glance away from the lens to think about the next thought, or even just a shift in eye focus that the lens can see to help give the impression that you are conversing, not just reciting.

### More Than One Camera

Live and live-on-tape[1] broadcasts are being used increasingly in corporate television in teleconferencing and other satellite situations. In these situations, you will probably be working with two or more cameras and will need to comfortably switch your focus from one camera to another on command if you are a host, moderator, news anchor, or spokesperson.

In these situations, it helps to think of each camera as an individual person. As you shift your attention from one camera to another, it's important to keep your movements as relaxed as your delivery is conversational.

Quick, jerky movements of the head or body as you shift from one camera to the other will not do. And try at all times to remember which camera is "on" you.

While these suggestions go almost without saying, you'd be amazed how many experienced television performers get (figuratively) caught with their pants down when a technician does an unannounced camera switch. The active camera will be revealed to you by the pointing finger of the floor manager or by the camera's tally light. The tendency is to focus on the right camera as fast as possible; but when switching translates into jerky movements and shifting eyes,

---

1. *Live-on-tape* means that the program is being shot without the benefit of retakes, even if mistakes are made.

the unforgiving camera will record the momentary panic and enlarge it in the eye of the viewer. This confusion drives directors batty in live situations because the error cannot be corrected in another take.

The best way to demonstrate your professionalism under this kind of fire, and in the process turn your director into a loyal fan, is to always remain relaxed, never move in a jerky manner, and slowly and smoothly turn to the correct camera *as if it were another person,* as if all of this was perfectly normal.

If you have notes in front of you, as you well might if you're in a corporate news program, the way out of losing-the-camera situations is even easier. As soon as you become aware that you are looking at the wrong camera, look down at your notes in a relaxed manner for a moment before turning to the correct camera.

Rest assured that this kind of situation happens frequently when there has been insufficient preproduction, a recurring problem in commercial as well as corporate television.

I recommend that *you* request in advance a list of planned camera changes, if such a list exists—or at least sit down with the director to try to determine when changes might occur to help eliminate problems and reinforce your air of professionalism. Often, prompter copy or scripts will be marked to indicate planned camera switches.

## Framing Considerations

There are several ways you can be framed by the camera: extreme close-up (ECU), close-up (CU), medium close-up (MCU), medium wide, or wide. Each way will affect your gestures, expressions, movements, and the way you hold a product or demonstrate activities or objects. Remember Web Lithgow's admonition? Generally speaking, the closer or "tighter" you are framed, the "smaller" you must work.

You must be sure that gestures occur on camera, not be-low the frame line. It will help if you always imagine yourself as inside a picture frame.

You also should be aware of situations that place chroma-keyed backgrounds or graphics and/or "boxes" be-side you in the frame. These devices add elements to the pic-ture that the viewer can see but you cannot.

The chroma-key is widely used where the talent—that's you—is placed in a scene shot by another camera. Visualize your local weather forecaster walking around on an elec-tronic weather map. We see the map as part of the scene, but in reality that map is physically not there. Your friendly fore-caster is actually shot in front of a blue background and just pretends the map is in the studio.

The "box" works the same way. The viewer sees a box which contains important information to the side of the nar-rator, but the narrator does not perform with that box. It's an electronic add-on. But it is vital that the talent know it's there and where it is placed in the shot. A box will, in effect, change the shape of your mental "picture frame."

### Gestures, Expressions, and Movement

It's natural to want to gesture for emphasis, but the medium of television demands that gestures be kept to a minimum and that repetitive gestures be avoided. Remem-ber, you don't want to do anything that breaks the intensity of the communication bond between you and the viewer by inserting unnecessary or attention-grabbing gestures. It's best to gesture *occasionally* but only when you are framed in a wide, medium-wide, or medium shot (see Figure 3.1). And as you work your way through a script, vary the kinds of ges-tures you use. Try using one hand, then the other, then both hands at once.

When you are in close-up your gestures must be exe-cuted slowly and with extreme care. In a close-up that is

**3.1** Illustration of wide, medium-wide, medium, close, and extreme close-up framing.

framed from the waist up or higher, working your hands into the shot is appropriate so long as they do not wave about too much and are clearly within the shot. This means that you must hold your hands higher than in wide or medium shots to ensure they're not halfway in the shot.

In head-and-shoulders shots, it is always best to gesture only with slight head motions. In extreme close-up, it's best to keep still with just your head showing.

The same general guidelines apply to facial expressions and movement. The farther away from the camera you are, the more realistic you should make your gestures and expressions. The tighter you are framed, the more you must minimize. In extreme close-up, for example, just the slightest movement of an eyebrow can say volumes about the way you feel. On the other hand, a large eyebrow movement may look out of place and "too big" for the situation, and be read as artificial by the viewer. You lose credibility when this happens.

The moral of all this, of course, is always to ask the director how you will be framed before each shot. And if multiple takes are used, you'll need to repeat gestures exactly from take to take for continuity. Who knows, the director might want to combine portions of takes in the final edit. So don't overdo it.

## Holding Product or Demonstrating

One of the most frequently performed tasks by on-camera spokespersons is the displaying of product and/or demonstrating how things work. These situations can be tricky at best.

Most of the time demonstration and product shots are accomplished with two cameras with one pointed at you in a medium-wide shot and the other at the product or object being demonstrated in close-up. Occasionally only one camera is used (see Figure 3.2).

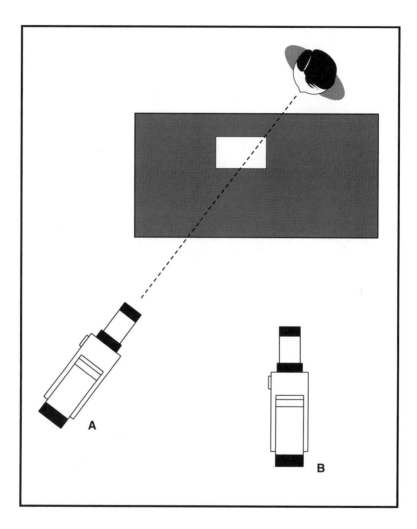

**3.2**  A two-camera setup for a product shot. Camera A shoots the talent while Camera B shoots what's on the table. You make eye contact with Camera A only in this arrangement.

With one camera, *you* have it easy. You'll first perform the demonstration in a medium-wide shot in which you'll go through your demonstration while making as much eye contact with the camera as possible. Once that shot has been completed to everyone's satisfaction, you'll do it again, this time with just the product or object in the shot. This one-camera approach is easy for you because in the close-up demonstration you do not have to look at the camera. You can focus your entire attention on holding the product or object.

A two-camera arrangement is much more difficult. Here, the medium-wide shot on you and the close-up on the object will be shot simultaneously. This means that you will have to double your concentration to maintain eye contact with one camera while holding the product still and at the correct angle (to avoid studio lighting reflections) for the other. This process can become triply difficult when you must progress through a series of complicated steps in a demonstration.

In such cases ask for plenty of rehearsal time to avoid unnecessary retakes. There is no question that all of your actions will be carefully thought out by the director, but you should remember that the director is not the actor in this situation. You are, and you need to be relaxed and comfortable with what you will do in order to give your best performance.

## Warnings

No, this does not mean that you are going to warn directors that they better treat you well and feed you on time *or else*. In this case, I am talking about warning the director or camera operator that you will do something unplanned while a live or live-on-tape shot is in progress.

You'd be surprised how often this predicament occurs during demonstrations and interviews or in taped lecture formats in which your situation calls for spontaneous movement of yourself or the object you must demonstrate.

To illustrate this, I'll walk you through a portion of a video I did for Maine's retirement system a few years back.

I was hired as a spokesperson to deliver a live-on-tape lecture to a large group of retirees about their retirement plan. A few actors who had been primed with questions to ask in a specific order had been planted in the audience of about sixty people.

As I delivered my memorized presentation, I made points, answered questions, and used a chalkboard for a visual aid. After consulting with the director, it was decided that I would "lead" the camera with both vocal and physical warning cues every time I went to the board.

Those cues included my saying something like "Let's go to the board" *before* I initiated the move to get there, and once I did initiate the move I did so very slowly and deliberately with an obvious shift of weight. This procedure gave the camera operator plenty of time to keep me in the shot as I crossed the floor. It also gave him time to change focus.

It's important that you understand that any unanticipated move you want to make should be handled with care and a warning in live or live-on-tape situations to help avoid camera miscues. Sophistication in this area will also enhance your professional reputation because you will be regarded as an actor who understands the problems your coworkers face.

## Role Playing in Dramatic Situations

In an industrial role-playing dramatic situation you play a character other than yourself, just as you would in a feature or a play. If you want to work you'll need to know how to develop a believable character.

Most industrial producer/directors want the dialogue memorized and expect you to be aware of the camera—without revealing that awareness to the viewer—at all times. Why? Because you never know what part of your body the director will shoot at any given time.

Because you have no control over shot selection, you must assume that your entire body is in the shot at all times and act accordingly. Every move and breath must be made for the camera as well as for the person or persons with whom you are acting, including your *actions* and your *reactions*.

Remember to keep everything small and understand that even a slight gesture or minimal facial expression goes a long way in close-ups, the shot of choice in industrial drama.

When working with other actors and following a prescribed script you must be extremely careful to follow all blocking instructions to the letter or you risk ruining shots the director has planned but has no time to fully discuss with you. Your coactors, too, will depend on your sticking to the script, both physically and verbally.

And consider that even when you know that another take is always an option, never stop a scene just because you feel like it. Ordering a cut is the director's job. If you feel uncomfortable with something, wait until the scene is completed and then suggest a retake with more comfortable action. If the director agrees that the scene can stand some improvement, another take will be in order.

The role-playing situation requires a different level of teamwork than does on-camera narration. Proper studio etiquette requires that you respect the work of others by leaving criticism up to the director and concentrating on your own performance exclusively. Don't try to stand out. You'll get more work if you are known as an actor who knows her or his place.

## On-Camera Audio Considerations

Whether you are cast as a spokesperson/narrator or as a dramatic performer, you must always be aware of audio. More industrial shoots have been sandbagged though audio foulups than any other single production category.

There are lots of things that can cause audio problems, but when you're the culprit you take the heat. Prepare yourself to avoid actor-related audio problems by practicing at home and by using a little common sense.

### Microphones

The first major audio consideration to understand is the kinds of microphones you're likely to encounter on a corporate shoot. The most frequently-used microphone is the *lavaliere microphone,* used for its superior sound reproduction quality, its small size, and its ease of concealment. This microphone is designed to be clipped to an actor's clothing such as a shirt or blouse or on the lapel of a jacket, with its wire hidden under the clothing (see Figure 3.3).

Problems usually arise with lavaliere microphones when the director requires that they be concealed under an actor's clothing or when the shoot is outdoors in windy conditions.

Concealment problems are associated with clothing contact and movement, and there are a couple of things you can do that will endear you forever to the audio engineers. First, wear all-cotton dress shirts and wool/cotton weave ties and neckerchiefs. These fabrics make less noise than silks and polyesters when they rub against microphones. Second, always be conscious of gesture and movement when wearing a concealed microphone and move with great care so that the area of clothing that conceals the microphone moves minimally.

Lavaliere mikes are almost always placed on your person by an audio engineer. You should expect a sound person to assist you in threading wires down pants and skirts as well as in and around shirts and blouses. Frequently, wireless transmitters will be taped by a sound person to parts of your body.

The second most commonly used microphone in the corporate environment is the *boom mike,* which is held

**3.3** Model Caroline Hendry is shown wearing a lavaliere microphone correctly placed just below the top button of her blouse.

above, below, or to the side of the camera shot by a boom mike operator. Problems may arise when you have to move. Several rules may help avoid pitfalls. First, move slowly so that the boom operator will be able to move with you and maintain the mike's distance from you. Second, never make an abrupt turn. Third, do not allow yourself to cut down the distance between you and the boom mike. Fourth, try to warn the boom operator before you make a move in the same way you warn the camera operator.

When turns are required, the boom mike operator may request that you speak, then turn, and then speak again to allow time for the microphone to be kept in the proper position.

The *hand-held microphone* is another common type. When you hold the mike in your hand, you are in complete control of audio and must follow a couple of standard procedures, which are, unfortunately, easy to forget. Make sure you have plenty of cable on hand with enough slack to enable you to move wherever you need to go without hindrance. Also, work out the position of the hand-held mike with the audio engineer and make sure that you find that exact position every time you speak.

When you are interviewing someone with a hand-held microphone, apply the same rule when pointing the microphone at the other person. Keeping the mike's position constant assures a consistently even audio level. It also makes the mike unobtrusive.

Sound pretty basic? As I said above, these rules are easy to forget under pressure. I remember running into trouble with a hand-held microphone during an important audition where my lack of concentration on mike placement lost me the job. I was in a major corporate studio interviewing mock corporate executives in stand-up style, and I kept forgetting to hold the mike steady in the same position in front of the interviewees' mouths. A simple error, but one large enough to give the producer the impression I was inexperienced, which at the time I most certainly was. I hope you won't make the same mistake.

**Studio Conditions**

**Noisy/Windy Environment**

**Incorrect Placement**

**3.4**  The correct and incorrect placement of hand-held micro-phones.

Another important rule to remember is to speak across the surface of the hand-held microphone and never directly into it. If the environment around you grows noisier you should hold the mike closer to your mouth (see Figure 3.4).

The *desk microphone* has one absolute rule: leave it alone once it has been placed by the audio engineer. You have other things to worry about. Remember as well to not pound the desk or rustle papers while speaking.

On shoots where all of the technicians work under union contract, you will not be permitted to touch any audio equipment except a hand-held microphone. Don't even think about it. Leave all adjusting and rearranging to audio personnel, even when it's obvious that you can accomplish the task in less time. It's just not worth alienating the powers that be.

## Audio Levels

Whatever microphone is in use, you must be aware of and adhere to the simple rules of *audio level* or sound volume. First, when asked to speak for the purpose of obtaining a level, use the same volume you plan to use during the shot. Second, don't pop your opening few words by overmodulating. This unconscious bad habit is one I've had to struggle with for years. And third, keep your volume level consistent throughout the shoot unless environmental conditions warrant otherwise.

## Energy Consistency

Do you find that you seem to have more energy early in the day than you do late in the afternoon? I know I do. Unfortunately, you can't let your energy fade on camera, even when you're heavily into overtime, which is a common corporate television occurrence. In other words, you must focus on your energy output throughout the shooting day and develop a few commonsense personal habits to ease the way.

Begin by taking care of yourself. Get plenty of sleep the day before the shoot, exercise regularly so you won't tire easily, and eat nutritious, healthy foods. Professional actors really have to be as physically conscious as athletes to withstand the pressures of the business and to project the almost universally positive images industrials demand. Red, baggy eyes and a pasty complexion will get you nowhere. You should be the picture of health and vitality to inspire confidence in others.

In addition, plan on reserving your energy throughout the shooting day or days until your strength is actually called for. When I was a kid, one of my football heroes was Jim Brown of the Cleveland Browns, an electrifying running back who later became a professional actor.

Brown had a habit of throwing everything he had into each run, then literally dragging himself up from the tackle and slowly returning to the huddle. I remember commentators drawing our attention to this habit time after time. After a while it was funny. But the practice really worked for Brown, and it can work for you.

During breaks, always try to go off by yourself, sit down, and relax. Meditate or read. Study your script if you need to. The important thing is to not expend too much energy socializing or being entertaining.

For an on-set helper, try this energy boost exercise—eight short staccato inhalations from the diaphragm, then eight exhalations through the mouth. Then four of each. Then two of each. Then one of each. Alternate closing nostrils and use the same eight, four, two, and one sequence for each side. That's three sequences. It works!

Now these suggestions may sound boring, but they make real sense if you know you'll have a long day or series of days. You want to look and sound as fresh in the last shot as you did in the first one. Don't forget that lots of projects are shot completely out of sequence, and the program's opening scene might be the last shot on a long day.

## Editing Considerations

Your timing, movement, and continuity are critically important as they apply to *editing,* which occurs after the shoot. In this process, the director and technicians assemble the best of the shots taken during the shoot into a final product.

Your knowledge of the film and video editing process will make or break you in this business because producers and directors need to feel confident that you won't do anything during the shoot that will cause them problems later. If you develop a reputation as someone who isn't aware of editing, no one will want to work with you because it's just too expensive to fix actor-related editing problems after the fact.

### Timing

There are several types of problems *you* have the potential to cause that show up in the editing room. I'll start with timing in dramatic role playing.

Editing room problems associated with actor timing are pegged to *stepping on lines,* a definite film and television industry no-no. When responding to your actor partners' cues, you must always leave room for an edit with a slight pause or beat, unless you are specifically instructed by the director to run the dialogue together, for situations such as close-ups and cutaways.

These slight pauses give the film or videotape editor breathing room to make clean shot selections, allowing each character to complete each section of dialogue while on camera without being overridden by another character. This also alleviates audio problems.

These slight beats make it difficult for the film and television actor to stay in character, but they are simply the nature of the beast. You will no doubt learn in your film acting courses that it's important to fill those beats and pauses with external business and internal moments to flesh out your character's intentions for the viewer. Just stopping and start-ing creates an unbelievable, stilted, and in the final analysis unacceptable character relationship.

## Movement and Continuity

Movement problems can drive editors crazy, and they most often occur when someone—usually the director or continuity person—forgets about the need to match progres-sive shots. Your reputation will be enhanced if you become known as an actor who thinks ahead.

In role-playing situations you should follow the block-ing set out for you by the director *to the letter* and make sure you start and stop your action in exactly the same manner in each take of the scene, which means *you* must be concerned with continuity.

For example, if at the close of scene one you are sitting with your left leg crossed over your right with your left hand resting in your lap and your right hand on the table grasping a pencil, then continuity demands that you match that posi-tion at the start of scene two. The rules of continuity require that someone remember the details of what you are doing from scene to scene in exact detail to aid the director and ed-itor when it comes time for post-production. This is usually the responsibility of a crew member, but your efforts to keep track of your continuity will be appreciated. You certainly don't want to be responsible for a reshoot, which could be the only alternative if continuity goes awry.

When you are a spokesperson or on-camera narrator, you should be very careful about camera turns and jump cuts. Most narrative programs involve shooting short sec-tions in sequence until the script is completed. You'll work a paragraph or two at a time. When you complete each sec-tion, a camera change will usually be made. You'll either be framed differently or the angle of the shot will be altered.

Framing changes involve either pulling you in closer, such as from a wide shot to a medium close-up, or pulling back. In either case you need to be very aware of your body position and the way you hold your hands so that abutting shots will match. You don't want to have your hand held chest high at the end of shot four and have it stuffed in your pocket at the start of shot five. The viewer needs to see you put it there at the start of scene five.

Head turns and body turns at the beginning and end of shots must also be accomplished with continuity in mind. If you are asked to turn to camera two position at the end of a shot, you will no doubt be asked to repeat that exact turn at the top of the next shot. This helps the shots match in the editing process and is a routine shooting procedure.

Sometimes routines get lost in the hustle and bustle of the often rushed and pressure-driven atmosphere of the industrial video environment. If the director does not seem to be paying attention to continuity factors, you should step in diplomatically with a subtle suggestion or two: "Do you want me to do that head turn at the top of this shot?" An astute director will probably agree and begin to think more about continuity in general.

Continuity problems are usually taken care of by a person hired for that express purpose, but this occurs only on high-budget shoots. When it comes to your character, you should always assume that continuity is your responsibility.

### Room Tone

Many inexperienced actors are caught off guard on the set when the director calls for *room tone*. Room tone is the sound the location of the shoot makes when all shooting activity is dead silent. Directors need room tone on tape during the editing process whenever there is a call for a pause to cover where some extraneous noise has inadvertently wound up on the tape. Taking a sixty-second pause for room tone is standard operating procedure, even in high-tech studios.

What does this mean for the actor? When the director calls for room tone, be absolutely still. Do not utter a sound. Breath as quietly as possible. After all, it's your microphone that will most likely be used to make this important audio recording.

## ✳ *Off-Camera Considerations*

The off-camera side of corporate television production requires that actors know their way around an audio booth by knowing who's who, what's expected, and what should be avoided in voice production. I will deal with this subject briefly here, but I recommend that you take a good voice-over class as part of your preparatory training.

You will rarely if ever work with more than a director and audio engineer in voice-over production. The director will be there to help you interpret the script, and the engineer will be concerned with the technical aspects of your performance, such as audio levels and articulation.

Again, I strongly recommend that you practice reading aloud for fifteen minutes every day to prepare for voice-over narration. Your reputation will be built not only on the quality of your voice and your interpretive ability, but on your reading proficiency as well.

### Your End of the Booth

As the industrial voice-over performer, you will be expected to read in a captivating fashion long scripts of material you may find boring. You must vary pitch, inflection, rate, volume, and timing. You will be expected to read scripts rather quickly, with great confidence, and with few flaws. Remember, however, that material that is boring to you is of *great* interest to the audience to whom it is targeted.

You may also be expected to read copy that does not fit its designated video segment, such as forty seconds of copy allotted only 29.4 seconds. Be patient. If the time frame is too short for the copy, the director will have to do an on-the-spot rewrite.

Although industrial voice work is akin to commercial sessions, there are significant differences. Commercial copy must be read to fit an exact time frame, but industrial jobs are rarely hampered by time. Most industrial work has been designed for audio cassettes, filmed documentaries, or videotapes that are not intended for broadcast.

Since the material is chiefly instructional in nature, industrial copy is often more straightforward than commercial copy. You should plan to be as conversational and energetically enthusiastic—without being hyper—as you can.

The average voice-over narration involves about fifteen to thirty minutes of copy, and you'll be asked to read such a document from beginning to end, stopping only for direction or when you make a mistake.

If you follow my at-home practice regimen, you'll soon get to the point where you can read a half hour of copy in under an hour, including time for stops for direction and flubs. The regimen will also give you the confidence to overcome the nervousness many beginning narrators face upon entering the unfamiliar confines of the audio booth.

It is always a good idea, of course, to request the script in advance, but producers expect voice talent to be able to read cold. If you arrive on a job without having seen the script, ask for some time to look it over to get a handle on its message before recording begins. Familiarity will help speed recording along because you won't have to stop as frequently to determine where to place emphasis, and you'll know how to pronounce those strange product names and acronyms.

When you reach the point of being able to walk into an audio booth with copy you've never laid eyes on and read it with perfect pace and variety and few mistakes, you'll be in top form.

# Personal Prompting Devices

Reading from a teleprompter is a skill. Some people do it better than others.

*— Carol Nadell*
*Selective Casting*

I don't like the earprompter. I hate it with a passion.

*— Don Blank*
*Georgia Pacific Television*

**R**eading from a teleprompter is most definitely a skill, and the earprompter is not everyone's friend, but these and other personal prompting devices are an industrial actor's bread-and-butter tools. You should know how to use them if you hope to carve out a niche as a business actor.

Don't plan to learn to use them on the job. Producers today expect actors to be well schooled in the use of prompting devices, and they become justifiably upset when someone who has problems in this area is hired. Let me illustrate.

Several years ago I was hired as a coanchor for a corporate news release. At the time my booking details were discussed, I was asked if I was *proficient* with an earprompter. I said I was. I'd been using them for a couple of years at that point and could handle long passages of copy with ease.

I remember quite clearly assuming in advance that this shoot would be a snap because my coanchor would no doubt be proficient with the earprompter, too. Wrong!

My coanchor arrived on the set with her brand new earprompter and not a shred of on-the-job experience or practice with this tricky device.

Needless to say, the shoot was a disaster. Take after take after take was ruined because of her unfamiliarity with the earprompter. And as time wore on the production crew grew increasingly frustrated, almost to the point of hostility. It was a difficult time for everyone involved, and all of the problems hinged on one simple actor error: lack of thorough preparation.

Now I'm sure that actress—an extremely talented performer—went home and practiced like mad to make sure she would never again be at fault with the earprompter. And I'm also sure that she is now advising all of her actor buddies that it is indeed unwise to show up on an industrial shoot without full preparation.

Industrial productions today are in many ways as sophisticated as commercial television. Projects are created for a generation of viewers who grew up with television as their primary resource and who are intolerant of anything less than high production quality. You, the actor, are expected to meet those standards.

Your ability with personal prompting devices is vitally important to your reputation as a reliable and efficient performer. I'll discuss prompting devices in detail so you'll be familiar with their quirks and can practice at home. *Even experienced actors who are inexperienced with prompters should read carefully.*

## ✳ Cue Cards

Cue cards? Yep, cue cards, also known as "idiot cards."

I'll bet you thought they went out with the Stone Age, but unfortunately they still lurk about the occasional corporate television studio. You are expected to be able to use them without looking as though you're using them, which is a tall order. They are, without question, the most awkward of prompting devices.

For those of you who have never encountered a cue card, a definition is in order. A cue card is a large card, usually made from poster board, on which is written the copy you are supposed to deliver. Although the copy is generally written by hand with a heavy felt-tip pen, sometimes cue cards will be adorned with stick-on letters. Unfortunately, this rarely occurs because the process is labor intensive. The size of the card and the lettering will depend on how far you are from the camera and on how well you can see.

Generally speaking, cue cards are used for short pieces of copy, but I've been on shoots in which an entire script, both narrative and dramatic, has been written on these difficult-to-use prompters.

They are onerous to all because they hinder the actor's eye contact with the camera lens in narrative situations, and they make it almost impossible to turn in a believable performance in a role-play.

Troubles most often arise when the card is poorly placed or the card holder improperly moves the card during a take or blocks portions of lettering with his or her hands.

When used in narrations, the cue card is placed beside the camera lens. But if the card holder does not butt the card up as close as possible to the lens, lateral eye contact prob-

**4.1** The correct placement of a cue card in a narration situation. Notice that the card is as close to the camera as possible. As you read, the card holder will raise the card to keep the copy adjacent to the lens.

lems associated with cue cards will be exaggerated (see Figure 4.1).

Let's say you're doing a ninety-second piece that has been carefully lettered by hand on three large cue cards held by an inexperienced card holder. That's right, *inexperienced.* Producers often give this kind of job to the least-competent person on the set, incorrectly assuming that it's something anyone can do with ease.

What's likely to happen? The cards will not be held in the proper location throughout the shot. As you read, the cards will have to be changed since there are three cards, and each card will have to be lifted steadily to keep the text aligned with the lens as you read along. The inexperienced card holder will have to do a juggling act to stay with your pace and not force you to look every which way to find the words you're supposed to be saying.

How can you lessen the damage this all-too-frequent scenario will have on the finished product? My best advice, when told you will be using cue cards, is to memorize the script. But if you can't do that, there are some simple steps to follow.

First, before you show up on the job ask what kind of prompting devices will be used. Second, request a copy of the script in advance. Third, become familiar with the script, almost to the point of memorization, before you arrive at the shoot. Fourth, train yourself to glance *only momentarily* at the cue cards each time you refer to them, giving the impression that your break from the lens is a natural one. If you really *look* at the cards, your act of reading them will be too obvious. And fifth, request several rehearsals so you and the card holder can coordinate comfortably with each other to ensure that the cards will be placed where they should be.

Does this sound like a lot of work? It sure is. It's too much work for the generally poor results because unless the camera lens is placed far enough away from you, there will always be noticeable lateral eye movement, which will break the desired communication bond between you and the viewer.

Similar problems occur in dramatic situations; the cards will be placed over the shoulder of the person or persons with whom you are playing the scene (see Figure 4.2).

The idea here is to maintain eye contact with the cards, not with the other actors. If the cards are placed correctly, the viewer will think you are looking at the other actors even though you are not. But if the cards are placed too far to the side of the other actors, your eye contact will appear

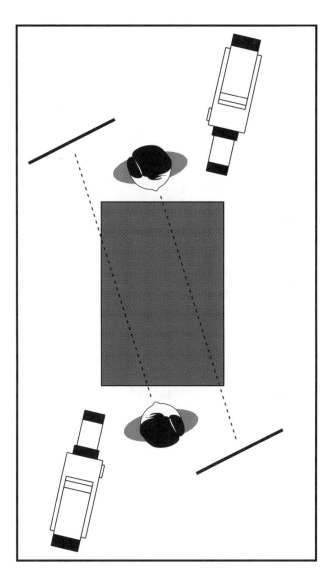

**4.2**   Two actors playing a scene with two cameras and using cue cards. Notice that the actors look at the cards and not at each other.

unnatural. In addition, the cards must be raised at your reading pace to keep the text at the eye level of the other actors in the scene.

Again, it's always better to memorize the role for a dramatic piece because that will help you internalize the character. Then you can make real eye contact with the other actors. The result will be a more believable scene.

If you have to use cue cards, ask for plenty of rehearsal, and remember to prepare at home to become as familiar with the script as you can. Preparation will help you when the card holder loses track of your pace or inadvertently covers your lines with his hands.

## ✳ *The Teleprompter*

The teleprompter is really nothing more than an electronic cue card, but its technology virtually eliminates many of the problems associated with paper cue cards. Although teleprompters are quickly becoming overshadowed in many parts of the country by the earprompter, teleprompters are considered by most producers and directors to be effective and productive prompting devices.

Like the cue card, teleprompters are most often used in narrative situations in which actors must wade through lots of copy in a relatively short period of time. Teleprompters are less frequently used in role-plays because directors rightly understand that they hinder believable dramatic performance.

Teleprompters, whether designed for the studio or the field, all work on the same principle: Lines of the script are projected and scrolled onto a clear glass plate angled directly in front of the camera lens. The lens looks through the clear glass plate at you. You look back at the lens, but instead of seeing the lens, you see the lines of the script projected on the glass plate in front of it.

In a studio teleprompter setup, the script is usually typed in oversized capital letters (or computer character-generated) onto a long sheet of paper placed on a variable-speed device that passes it in front of a camera. The script image is then relayed to a monitor set on the camera. The image on the monitor is then reflected onto the glass plate from which you read (see Figure 4.3).

The speed of the script scrolling before its camera is in most cases controlled by the teleprompter operator, but sometimes you will get to do that for yourself while you narrate.

The field teleprompter works a little differently because it is self-contained. The script is printed onto rolls that turn as you read, and the image is reflected onto the glass plate in front of the lens using mirrors. Its intended use is exactly the same as the studio teleprompter, but it is designed for one camera only, making it impractical for role-plays.

You should understand that the teleprompter is used extensively in industrials because it is a real time saver on budget-restrictive projects.

Remember that industrial directors routinely shoot pages and pages of copy—usually entire scripts—in just one day. They *have* to work quickly, and that means you must be efficient.

Most experienced producers and directors know that memorizing scads and scads of copy, particularly copy that's loaded with industry-specific jargon, is difficult for anyone. They also know that memorization mistakes are inevitable. That's why the teleprompter—even with its inherent faults—has become an accepted alternative in narrative programs that guarantees efficiency as long as a performer knows how to use it.

Problems associated with performers and teleprompters are usually due to print quality, distance, and scroll timing.

If you can't see the script, you can't read it, right? Before you hear "Action!" work out the placement of the camera

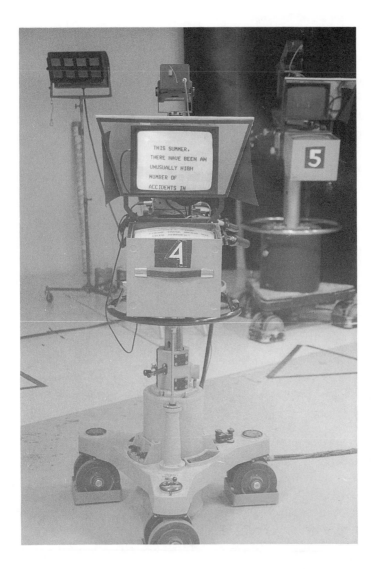

**4.3**  A studio camera with a teleprompter monitor set on the camera. The image on the monitor is reflected on the glass plate above. You see the image, in this case your script, instead of the camera's lens.

with the director. The camera should be close enough so you can easily see the print without squinting, but not so close as to make your eyes move from side to side while reading. If this kind of compromise proves impossible, you may need corrective lenses (assuming that the script is clearly printed, typed, or computer generated).

Timing problems should be worked out with the teleprompter operator in rehearsal so that you can read at your natural pace. As you read, the line of script you speak should always be centered on the lens. Also, script changes and special emphasis should be written in on the rolls or entered into the character generator.

Always prepare for the teleprompter at home by becoming very familiar with the script. Know what you will read and where emphasis should be placed. Practice reading the script aloud several times, which will help you overcome potential flubs due to an inattentive teleprompter operator.

In studio role-playing situations, teleprompted television monitors are placed over the shoulders of the actors playing the scene in much the same manner as cue cards. All of the actors see the entire script—not just their lines—as it passes through the teleprompter. All you need to do is read your lines as they pop up on the screen (see Figure 4.4).

As with cue cards, never look at your acting partner. Play all of your lines and your reactions to your partner's lines to the teleprompted monitor. If you shift your eyes from the teleprompter to the actor with whom you are conversing, your eye movement will tip off the viewer that you are using a prompting device, and the world of the scene will be violated.

As I mentioned earlier, many corporate producers and directors refuse to allow teleprompters in role-playing situations because they feel spontaneity is lost. You can help avoid stilted readings by practicing with the script (which you've requested in advance) at home. The last thing you want to do is show up on the job and do a cold reading.

**4.4**   In this role-playing situation Harriet Dawkins finds her lines on the teleprompter, which she sees over Tom Power's left shoulder.

## ✳ *The Earprompter*

The earprompter holds several advantages over cue cards and teleprompters. It is now considered the prompting device of choice in narrative situations among most producers and directors interviewed for this book. But those same people feel that it just doesn't work as well as memorization in dramatic scenes.

Earprompters fall into two categories, wireless and manual.

## Wireless Earprompters

Technically defined, a *wireless* earprompter is a "telcoil only" hearing aid unit that has no environmental microphone to receive external signals. It only receives induction signals through a neck loop.

In layman's terms, the wireless earprompter is a tiny flesh-colored earpiece that fits into your ear canal just like a hearing aid. It has a built-in receiver and comes with a neck loop that plugs into a microcassette recorder. When you play the recorder, the earpiece picks up the signal and you hear the recording (see Figure 4.5).

Because the earprompter fits inside your ear, it is considered *completely personal equipment.* This means that an earprompter will not be provided for you by the producer. It's something you'll have to purchase for yourself.

It's also expensive, so before you run out and buy one there are several things to consider. You'll need to determine if you can use it competently and whether or not your future casting potential warrants the investment.

Let's see how it works in a narrative situation. You first hide the neck loop under your clothing with just the connector jack available to plug into the cassette recorder. Then you record the first on-camera section of the script into the tape recorder, employing a three- to five-second delay at the top of the tape, at a pace determined by the director. Do not record the entire scipt into the tape recorder in advance, because pace considerations and possible last-minute script changes will invariably result in your rerecording everything anyway. It's always best to progress shot by shot.

At this point you have a couple of options. You can read the copy interpretively with performance-level energy, or you can read it in a flat monotone.

I recommend reading it flatly at the desired pace to allow you to play with interpretation and energy from take to take. Because you hear the script without emphasis—just the words—you will not become distracted by the strong

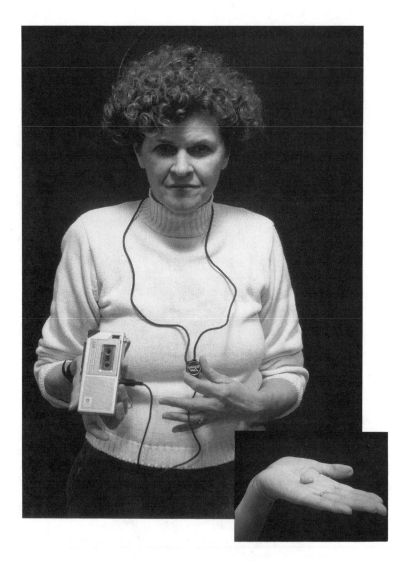

**4.5**  Caroline Hendry wears a neck loop that is plugged into a microcassette recorder. On a shoot, the neck loop would be worn under her clothing and the tape recorder concealed in a pocket. The wireless earprompter (inset) goes in her ear.

suggestions in a prerecorded interpretation. When you become comfortable using this device, you will have developed your own best method of employing it, which may include reading with interpretation. But for now, begin by reading it flatly.

Once you have recorded the appropriate section of script with a delay at the top of the tape, you simply rewind the tape, plug the neck loop into the recorder's ear jack, conceal the recorder in a pocket, and press the play switch when you hear "Action!" You'll hear silence during the delay and then your voice delivering the recorded script. You then speak the words you hear—with appropriate energy and interpretation—at a two- or three-word delay. If the volume of what you're hearing isn't quite right, simply adjust the volume control on the tape recorder or on the earpiece, if a volume control or "intensity wheel" is provided on your model.

The three- to five-second time delay you've recorded at the top of the tape is important to give you time to adjust your clothing and make an initial move or head or body turn before you speak. You also need time to get your body in position after turning on the tape. Just explain your time delay requirements to directors who are unfamiliar with the earprompter.

If the section of copy you've recorded has built-in pauses for action or graphics, you should rehearse using the script a couple of times. You should time out the pauses with the director using a stopwatch—a piece of equipment *you* should bring to the shoot. Then record the copy with the timed-out pauses included. If you use a consistent pace on every take, everything should be timed to perfection. If not, you'll have to become consistent to use the earprompter efficiently.

Dramatic situations are another matter. Certainly the earprompter *can* be used in role-plays. In fact, it quite frequently is, but the system has disadvantages when it comes to timing.

As Don Blank of Georgia Pacific Television puts it, "Acting is a matter of timing. You can't develop the flow of a character with an earprompter because you can't interact on a human level with another actor when using it. Once you lay that copy down into the earprompter, you're going to spit it out the way it's coming into your ear."

This makes complete sense; to turn in a believable performance you have to act and react based upon what you're given by the other actor or actors. You have to honestly respond to the stimuli you receive, not send out canned words. The earprompter does make genuine acting difficult.

But with the right amount of rehearsal, proper recording technique, and the opportunity of working with actors who are also using the earprompter, you can certainly perform as competently in dramatic scenes as you would using the teleprompter.

There are two ways to go with recording technique. You can record all of your lines and only your acting partners' cue lines into your recorder. Then, using a pause switch, you play the scene.

Let's say, for illustration, that you have the first line. What you'll hear in the earprompter at first is *your line* followed immediately by your next line's *cue*. After you say your line and hear your cue on the tape, you pause your tape until your acting partner says the cue line. Then you release the pause switch to hear your next line and cue, and so on down through the scene. This method requires that you use a tape recorder that has a remote jack, into which is plugged the pause switch.

The other method is for you and your partners to record the entire scene together into your tape recorders. Then, when you play the scene you will not need a pause switch because you will not only hear all of *your* lines, but all of your partners' lines as well. You can well imagine, I'm sure, that timing inconsistencies from take to take make this recording method chancy. All it takes is for one of you to change the timing on one line and everyone will become lost immediately. Again, if there are pauses built into the script for action or graphics, you'll need to build them into your recording.

Whatever recording method you choose, lots of rehearsal is recommended, particularly if you are inexperienced with the earprompter. Even seasoned pros have to bring all their concentration skills to bear to make the earprompter work in dramatic situations. And most of them will tell you that their performances are not up to par with memorization.

When purchasing a wireless earprompter make sure to avoid the generic ones often advertised through mail order companies. They usually have audio problems because they are not molded to your ear. Sound will leak from them as you perform unless the volume is turned down very low, which makes it difficult for you to pick up your lines over the sound of your natural voice.

Purchase wireless earprompters though reputable hearing aid specialists and audiologists to get top-quality units and fair warrantes. And insist that your earprompter have an ear mold made from your ear to ensure that there will be no sound leakage and only you will hear the prompter.

Take this book with you when ordering an earprompter. Have the hearing aid person read this section so that there will be no misunderstandings.

## Manual Earprompters

Manual earprompters work exactly the same way as wireless earprompters in terms of their use by the actor, but they differ in how they interface with the tape recorder.

A manual system is one that has a custom "behind the ear" ear mold with a long hollow tubing that fits under your suit coat collar, shirt, or blouse. The tubing is connected to a receiver adapter and a button receiver, with a cord that goes from the button receiver to an earphone plug that fits your tape recorder's output or ear jack (see Figure 4.6).

Sound complicated? Not really. Take this description to a hearing aid specialist and they'll know what to do. Again, make sure that the earpiece is custom molded to your ear!

Also make certain they understand the necessary impedance match, which is the balance of the loudness of the sound coming from the tape recorder to the ear mold. In other words, the button receiver must have the same impedance as the recorder's output. It's a good idea to bring your tape recorder with you.

The manual earprompter is a good place to start if money is a concern, because manual units cost about one-third less than a wireless unit. On the other hand, you'll need to get one for each ear because you won't be able to reveal the cord going from the earpiece into your collar when you are shot from the side.

It is important to remember that when you're shot from the side, the camera will be able to see what's in your ear and the cord leading to the tape recorder. You must have another custom-molded earpiece for your other ear, which the camera can't see. With a manual earprompter for each ear you'll be ready for every eventuality.

## Backups

I have two wireless earprompters (one is a backup in case of a mechanical breakdown) and two manual earprompters that I use in stationary situations for two reasons. My manual units save wear and tear on the more expensive wireless units, and they have better audio quality. I recommend that you have backups for everything—jacks, pause switches, even tape recorders—because if something goes down during a shoot, you're responsible.

The last thing you want to have happen is for the cast and crew to lose a portion of a day because your equipment

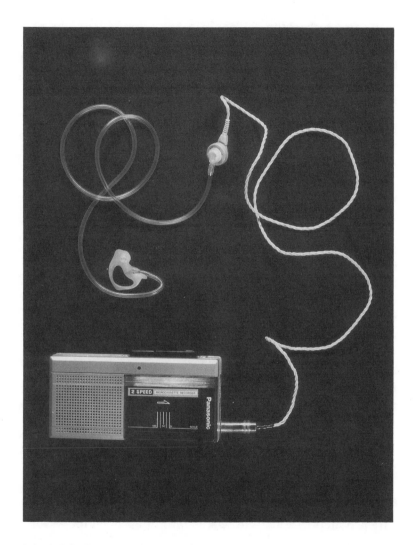

**4.6** With the manual earprompter, a custom "behind the ear" ear mold is connected by a hollow tubing to a button receiver, which is connected by a wire to an earphone jack, which plugs into your tape recorder.

fails. Having backups will also impress your coworkers and tell them that you are a professional performer who is prepared for the unexpected.

## Advantages of the Earprompter

For producer and performer, the earprompter's advantages over cue cards and teleprompters are many, providing you know how to use it well.

Producers and directors love the system in narrative situations because it saves them time and money and gives them greater shot selection flexibility.

Time is saved because the narrator/spokesperson will not make as high a percentage of flubs as with memorization, and fewer takes will be shot to arrive at a "keeper." In addition, the narrator can assimilate on-the-spot script changes in a matter of seconds by using the shot-by-shot technique of recording into the earprompter.

Ask any narrator who's memorized a twenty-page corporate script what it's like to make on-the-spot script alterations, and you'll learn that it's a time-consuming process. It's not easy to do. In fact, with some of the more technical scripts inherent in corporate television, it's next to impossible.

I've been in that situation plenty of times, but since I've learned how to use the earprompter, script changes have ceased to be a problem. The earprompter not only saves the producer time, it saves the performer time and effort as well. In addition, money is saved because time is money in corporate production and because a teleprompter operator will not have to be employed.

The earprompter also saves money in dramatic scenes when dragging along complicated teleprompter equipment is impractical and multiple script changes are anticipated. But, again, memorization remains the prompter of choice in role-plays.

Show me a producer who doesn't want to save money. For monetary reasons alone, your ability with the earprompter is a great selling point for you.

But an earprompter also sells for creative reasons. When an actor is tied to a teleprompter the camera must be close enough to be clearly seen. With the earprompter, the camera can be anywhere, which is particularly important on remote shoots. Imagine trying to see the teleprompter in bright sunlight when the camera is (by necessity) over fifty feet from you. It can't be done without memorization or the earprompter.

Another creative advantage is that the earprompter virtually eliminates the lateral eye movement and glassy stare associated with the teleprompter, and it allows the narrator to interact naturally with her or his environment.

Earprompters are also wonderful for actors who perform in live trade shows and must memorize somewhat lengthy and often highly technical information.

## Is the Earprompter for You?

The earprompter is a very popular and versatile device, but you need to determine if you really need one before you go to the expense of buying one. You should also learn whether you can use it efficiently.

You should first ask yourself when you contemplate making the investment if you are a good narrator/spokesperson or news anchor type. If not, forget the earprompter. If the answer is yes, read on.

Assuming you have the potential to be using the earprompter enough to justify its cost, you should test yourself with a generic earprompter to see if it works for you. Go to any electronics store near you and purchase an inexpensive audio tape recorder that has a listening or ear jack and purchase an earpiece to go along with it—one of those "private listening devices" that often comes with tape recorders.

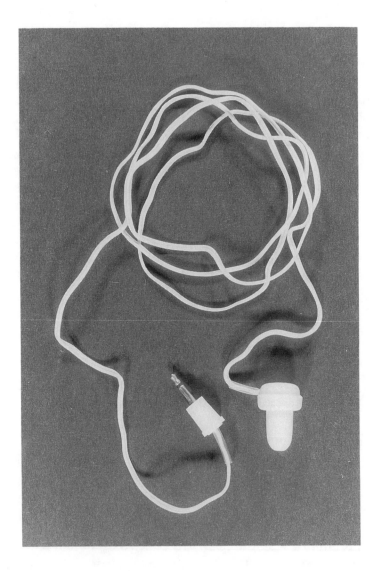

**4.7**   With an inexpensive, generic earpiece you can practice using an earprompter with your tape recorder for very little cost.

Better yet, borrow the tape recorder from a friend and buy the earpiece (see Figure 4.7).

Then practice in the privacy of your home. First, record a few sentences from one of those *Wall Street Journal* articles you've been reading, stick the generic earpiece in your ear, and play it back. Try to speak along with it. You will no doubt find yourself speaking gibberish in very short order. But don't give up. Repeat the process several times until you get it right. Then keep repeating it until you feel confident you can do this small piece of copy in your sleep.

Then try a little longer piece of copy. It shouldn't take too much time to determine whether you can actually master the basic process, but your prepurchase practice sessions should include more than just the technical process of spitting out the recorded message. Add interpretive changes to your recordings. Try reading onto the tape at faster and slower speeds and at higher and lower energy levels. Work with emphasis.

In other words, try to give yourself the kind of script interpretation direction you're likely to receive on an actual shoot and see if you can adapt to it while using the earprompter. If you can (and you'll know if you can't), go to a hearing aid specialist (remembering to take this book with you) and purchase one. Once you start working, you'll never regret it. And if you're already working, you'll soon see that the earprompter can change your life. It's certainly changed mine.

# Business Headshots
and Resumes

How do you get me to take an initial interest in you? By
having incredibly good headshots.

*— Nancy Doyle*
*Casting Director*

Your business headshot should say not only that you're
pleasant and friendly, but also that you mean business.

*— Lynn Wayne*
*Photographer*

**N**ancy Doyle's advice to actors is important; the
headshot is your major promotional tool. But it's not your
only important tool.

Both this chapter and the next chapter will explore
these tools from a business point of view, one which may not
always agree with more theatrically motivated forms of actor
promotion.

While I'm sure you've received plenty of professional
advice and have read lots of books and articles on self-adver-
tising for stage and screen actors, it's essential to look at the

process with an industrials focus if you want to succeed in this corner of the acting world. And why shouldn't you want to do just that? Remember, the industrial/nonbroadcast arena is the fastest-growing segment of the acting business in terms of jobs and dollars!

## ✳ Headshots

There is a school of thought that says a good commercial headshot is all you need to attack *all* segments of the acting business ranging from theater to trade shows. I hope to persuade you that having a headshot targeted directly to industrials will increase the percentage of jobs you land.

Remember the discussion on developing a businesslike point of view in the chapter on preparation? The same rationale applies to your promotional tools. They should reflect that point of view, be conservative, and as Lynn Wayne puts it, "Say that you mean business." You need a business headshot, which could potentially double as your commercial headshot if you are the spokesperson type.

Regardless, there are several points to consider when acquiring a business headshot.

- Choosing the right photographer
- Preparing for the photo session
- Developing the right attitude during the shoot
- Choosing the right photograph

### The Elements of a Good Business Headshot

The single most important element of *any* headshot is that *it must show what you're going to look like* when you walk in to the audition, interview, job, or whatever.

Your business headshot *must* meet this test. And while we're on the subject of looks, it's important to understand that your looks have plenty to do with whether or not you will be cast. In order to work regularly in the corporate environment you must at least have a generic business image, which today does *not* mean you have to look like the completely polished, perfect professional spokesperson. Today, most industrials employ regular-looking believable people—people with whom employees and customers can identify. If you have really unusual looks, however, steady industrial work may be hard to come by.

But the business headshot should say something more about you than just how you look. It should show something that will give you an edge in the corporate environment. That something is very subtle and goes beyond your type and whether or not you are "right" for the job under consideration.

Think for a moment about the difference between a portrait and a headshot. What comes to mind when someone says they're going to get their portrait done? If you're like me you immediately assume they're going to go to a portrait studio where the photographer will shoot five or six frames against a somewhat dreamy background while the subject poses while looking off into the distance. The result will be a romantically motivated beauty shot. A headshot, on the other hand, tries to capture your personality in a positive way. It's very specialized.

Casting people want to see a good representation of you that's not overly moody, contrived, or funny, but that *does* indicate that you are a pleasant person. Given these conditions, what should the business headshot say about you?

Every producer, director, casting person, and professional photographer interviewed for this book agrees that a business headshot should say that you're friendly, approachable, easy to work with, and confident. And the way to make these people feel good about you when they look at your photograph is to be relaxed and confident during the photo session, which any actor will tell you is not necessarily the easiest thing to do.

Whether you are approaching industrials as an actor who wants to be a spokesperson or a role-player, your ability to communicate a successful message in your headshot hinges on choosing the right photographer.

## Choosing the Right Photographer

If you live in or near a major city, you should have no difficulty finding a reputable professional photographer who specializes in headshots. There probably will be several in large cities. But how do you choose the right one, the one who understands the importance of your headshot and what it should say to your business-oriented prospects? This is a tough call for any actor.

If you're just starting out or are new to a particular area, the obvious strategy in locating competent photographers is to ask around. Begin by calling or dropping by (dropping by is best, because out of simple politeness they'll be more likely to pay attention to you) the local SAG, AFTRA, or Actor's Equity Association office and ask for the names of reputable headshot photographers in the area. You will probably get names but not recommendations from the union offices. If there are any actors hanging about, and there frequently are, ask them for names, too.

If you strike out at the union offices, go to local professional theaters, talent agencies, and casting agencies to ask for recommendations. Look at their bulletin boards for advertisements. It makes sense that any reputable agent or casting director will only allow photographers whose work they support to advertise on their walls. While there, ask any actors you see for their recommendations.

Don't shop for a photographer through the yellow pages, and don't assume that just because photographers

advertise in *Backstage, Variety,* or any other entertainment industry publications that any of them will be the one for you.

## A Warning

Be wary of the agency headshot scam. Even though this
chapter assumes that you have at least some vicarious or real
experience in the field of professional acting, beginners need
to be skeptical of those casting and talent agents who just
want to take your money. These people *are* out there, and if
you're the type of person who lets ego dominate common
sense, then—cliches aside— you're also fair game to be taken
to the cleaners.

Most photo scams work this way: The aspiring professional actor drops into an agent's office after responding to
an ad in the local paper seeking actors and models. The actor
is told that success is right around the corner. "What a great
type!" our actor is told. "All you need is some great headshots, and we'll represent you." And then the catch. The actor has to go to *their* photographer and pay an outrageous
price for the session and multiple prints. Forget it. The
minute you hear this kind of ploy from a talent or casting
agent, run—don't walk—the other way. Recommendations
by union offices, working actors, and professionals in the
field are the only way to go.

Depending on your location, you'll probably receive
several names and have no idea which one to select. Your
best approach is to narrow the field to at least three recommended photographers. Although it sounds obvious, choose
the three whose names pop up the most frequently. Then see
them, check out their work, and ask lots of questions.

Looking at the prospective photographer's work should
be your first task. You'll probably be shown a large portfolio
or two of recent headshots to review. As you flip through the
photos, look for business shots. Pay close attention to the
lighting; you don't want heavy shadows that put circles un-

der your eyes or have half of your face in deep shadow. You want a well lit and nicely contrasting black-and-white shot, one that positively but not dramatically reveals the natural contours of your face and, perhaps, a little of your upper body.

Pay very close attention to the eyes, because they are the most important element of a headshot. They should be alive and reveal intelligence and warmth, but everything else in the photograph should be clear and clean.

If you like the photographer's work, then it's time for questions. Start with technical and business matters.

- *What will be the background for the picture?* It should be light to medium gray. You do not want high-drama lighting here.

- *Does the photographer shoot in head-and-shoulders composition as well as the traditional format?* The answer should be yes, and you might consider having both a traditional headshot and a head-and-shoulders shot taken during the session. Both formats are now accepted by most casting people nationwide, and you might look considerably better in one or the other (see Figure 5.1).

- *How much film will be shot?* Two rolls of thirty-six exposures each, minimum, is what you'll need.

- *Who will own the negatives?* You want to own the negatives, don't you? You paid for them, after all. Some photographers will balk at this, so choose another photographer or negotiate. Owning your own negatives will be a plus when you want to place photo ads down the road, because you won't have to ask for the photographer's permission or pay a fee to use the negatives.

- *What will the photo session cost?* This is a tough one, and there is no single or correct answer. You certainly

**5.1**   These five corporate headshots show a range of looks that are appropriate for the corporate actor. Janice Wayne's and Ted Norton's headshots are clearly the most "corporate," followed by Linda Carole Pierce, Cope Murray, and Polly Cottam.

want the best value for your money but, considering the importance of your headshot, you cannot afford to sacrifice quality. The best advice is to not have it done cheaply. If you can afford the session, you love the person's work, and all other questions have been answered to your satisfaction, go for the very best, even if it costs the most. But again, ask around to discover a ballpark rate for headshots in your area to avoid being overcharged.

- *How many prints are included in the session fee?* Usually just one. Try to negotiate more, because you'll want more to make a final decision.

- *Is a make-up artist required? If so, how much will that cost?* Be wary of costly requirements. Men don't usually need make-up other than a little powder to blot shine, and women shouldn't go overboard. Women should be familiar with their own make-up and should be ready to do touch-ups for the photograph with the word *understatement* always in mind. Learning how to do make-up that's appropriate for film and television, as well as for photo sessions, is part of your general preparation.

  The downside of a professional make-up artist for your photo session is that the artist will put make-up on you that you won't know how to duplicate on the day of your interview or audition. You won't look like your headshot when you walk through the door since you won't be able to imitate that professional make-up job on an everyday basis. You're going to have a beautiful, glamorized picture of yourself, yes; but if you have lines and wrinkles on your face, the casting people need to see that in your headshot. Remember, this isn't modeling. They're not looking for perfect faces.

  On the other hand, if you have a blemish that won't be there every day, you should cover that up.

But don't cancel the shoot for a blemish, unless you're unusually broken out.

- *Are there any guarantees or refunds if you're not satisfied?* Be wary of the photographer who says "Take it or leave it." One of the intangible things you're trying to ascertain from your interview is whether or not you feel comfortable with this person. A tough, businesslike manner in what you hope will be a productive relationship may work against you when the shooting starts.

  Most reputable photographers will take more shots if you're not satisfied. It's unreasonable to demand a refund, however, unless the work is obviously below the standards of the photographer's work with other actors.

- *How long will you have to wait before seeing contact sheets and final prints?* One week for contact sheets and another week for final prints is standard.

- *Will you have to pay cancellation fees and/or deposits?* Many photographers require cancellation fees and deposits, but you should negotiate to keep these dollar amounts to 25 percent or less of the session fee. There should be cancellation fees for cancellations made *only* within forty-eight hours of the session.

Asking all of the above questions up front will help you avoid unpleasantness later. And don't worry, good photographers like to get everything out in the open, too. They'll appreciate your cautious approach to photographer selection.

Once you have the business and technical questions out of the way, try to find out about the photographer's understanding of business headshots. Ask such leading questions designed to get a photographer to talk about corporate work as, "What's the key ingredient in a business headshot?" or "What should the business headshot say to the viewer?" Listen carefully to the responses.

You want to work with a photographer who not only understands what you need but also takes you seriously. Sadly, too many "creative" headshot photographers put corporate shots down; you don't want to hire these photographers.

Assuming all questions have been answered to your satisfaction, make your selection based upon personality. Choose the photographer with whom you feel most comfortable, the one with whom you feel you can really be yourself. This is most important, because as you know by now, it's your self the headshot must reveal.

Once you've decided on the right photographer and set up an appointment, you'll need to think about getting ready for the photo session.

## Preparing for the Photo Session

You need to do several things to prepare for your photo session to insure that you will look your best and build your confidence. Remember, the subtle message you want your headshot to convey is extremely important.

### Practical Preparation

I know I'm not your mother, but *practical* preparation involves getting plenty of sleep for at least a few days before you have your headshot taken. You'd be surprised how many headshots display unnecessary circles under those very important eyes. To promote a healthy glow, try eating right and exercising regularly!

If you think this appeal is for beginners only, guess again. A few years ago, during one of those career transitional periods when things get slow and the phone never seems to ring, I decided that a new headshot was in order. I had aged three years since my last one anyway, and the time seemed right. So I went to a very good photographer and had it done. I was very excited by the positive vibrations going on during the shoot and knew a really great headshot would be forthcoming.

When my contact sheets arrived my spirits continued to soar. There were so many usable choices! But when my eight-by-ten prints showed up about a week later, I immediately knew the entire session would have to be repeated. The eyes were wrong. I looked tired in the blow-ups. Those circles just wouldn't do. Moral: If it can happen to me it can happen to you. Get some sleep. Live healthily.

Another basic for men is to get a haircut about a week before the session so that your hair doesn't look freshly cut. Women shouldn't style their hair specifically for the headshot. Instead, style your hair the way it will be worn to all future auditions using the new headshot. Again, the point here is that you must always look like your headshot when you walk in.

To elaborate on this last point for a moment, remember that you'll need a new headshot every time your look changes. A change in hairstyle often is far more expensive than the cost of the cut alone. For women, I recommend staying away from short, trendy styles. Go for something midlength that you can work with to create both trendy and traditional looks as appropriate.

For the photo session, be traditional, but pull your hair back a little so the camera can see your face. Think about it: If you've got wildly permed hair and you're wearing a business suit, they might not match. Men and women both need to keep in mind that hair should be more businesslike to appeal to a conservative audience. You don't want a pony tail for a corporate shot.

Another preparatory basic issue is to decide what to wear and have it cleaned and pressed in advance. Plan on bringing at least three business-oriented outfits with you to the session, keeping in mind the points raised about business attire raised in chapter 2.

Recommended suit colors are banker's gray, blue, and charcoal pinstripe. Having lighter and darker suit selections will be a real plus when it comes down to choosing shots from contact sheets. Some men with light or graying hair might need the contrast of a darker suit; someone with dark features might need a lighter one. Bringing both to the session will insure that those possibilities will be met. Choose all-wool suits for texture, and pastel rather than white dress shirts to help with contrast. Button-down collars are alright.

Women should bring a variety of pastel blouses, preferably in silk, and wool suit jackets. Simple, understated jewelry is fine. Try pearl stud earrings if nothing else seems right. Bring along some silk scarves for accent purposes, but nothing too busy or frilly. You're a woman who means business. If you just can't figure out what to wear, thumb through a few issues of *Fortune* or *Business Week* or watch a business channel on cable television and see what women wear on the job. Remember, though, that the camera doesn't like wild contrasts, and *you* want to stand out, not your clothes.

### Personal Preparation

You will also need *personal* preparation if you are new to the camera. As a general rule, people who have worked in front of the camera or who have taken on-camera classes link up with the camera more quickly that those who have not.

It's very important that you do everything you can to ensure that you will connect with the camera to have a successful session. But it isn't easy. Many if not most actors are afraid of having their headshots taken. You are showing your "self" after all, not some character in a script. Headshots can be a real risk. What if you don't like yourself as revealed by the camera?

Well, no one can ensure that you will like the way you look in your headshots, but you can go a long way to ensure that they will present a fair and honest representation of you. Assuming you're healthy, rested, and properly dressed, you now have to find a way to be yourself in front of the camera. And that, for beginners, requires some practice.

All of the photographers I've interviewed suggest that you get some advance practice at home working with inanimate objects and trying different types of smiles in front of a mirror as a substitute for the camera. In your practice sessions pretend that the camera is another person, someone with whom you're having a conversation. Then carry that idea into the session.

Sure, the photographer will be there to help you relax and "find yourself." But because headshots are so important and because this is your calling card we're talking about, it's a good idea to get your concentration going in advance. Preparation will enhance your confidence, and you'll project that in your finished headshot.

## During the Shoot

Your attitude during the shoot is everything. And even if you are as positive and confident as you want that face in your headshot to be, some things tend to get in the way. Unlike the television camera, which records you in action, the headshot camera environment is much more contained and stilted. You're not moving in front of the camera, and you're sucking all of your personal energy into your face.

It makes sense to expect that you'll need time to relax and that most of the first roll of film will be just for practice. This is a good reason to choose a photographer who shoots lots of film. If you have chosen a photographer with whom you feel comfortable and whom you trust, after a while you should begin to have fun. Your best shots will come when you hit this stage.

General guidelines for expressions are simple. First of all, you don't want to be big and grinny and smiley in a corporate shot. Be more down to business. If you want a smiling shot you want to be pleasant and approachable but not goofy. If you want a serious shot, you want to be serious, but not hard and cold. It should have a friendly quality.

Most business headshot photographers recommend going for some shots with teeth, but not exaggerated grins.

Most actors working in corporate television today are older—in their late thirties or their forties, fifties, or even sixties. Younger actors who want to penetrate the corporate arena should play up their age in their headshots by not trying to look so youthful. Younger folks should stay away from big, youthful grins because it's very rare that you see business people of any age doing that. People who are in power—or who want to be in power—don't walk around being overly expressive. They don't put all of their cards on the table at once.

## Choosing the Right Photograph

A few days after the photo session your contact sheets should be ready, and you'll be looking at 72 or, better yet, 108 tiny pictures of yourself. Now what will you do? How will you choose? Be careful. You don't want to pick one you like but others say looks nothing like you. And you don't want to pick one that *you* don't like either.

Here's a workable approach: Using a magnifying glass, or 8x loupe, look at all the pictures at one sitting and pick the half-dozen shots you like best. Ask people in the business, people you trust—acting coaches, casting directors, agents, other actors you respect, the photographer who took your picture—to help you decide. I do this every time I have a new headshot taken.

Have them look at all the pictures and pick the six shots *they* like best. The ones that both you and a majority of your helpers approve of are probably all going to be workable.

Whatever you do, don't mark the six you like best on the contact sheets since this may bias your helpers. Instead, note your favorite shots by row and number within the row. In fact, for your helpers' sake, you can number the vertical and horizontal rows so they, too, can give you a list. For example, a typical listing would be third row, fourth from left.

Let's say you've narrowed the field to three. Before you make your final selection, ask the photographer to print the finalists in an eight-by-ten format, toned for reproduction by a photo service. You may have to fork out additional money for some of these prints, but it's well worth it.

Sometimes an eight-by-ten blow-up looks a lot different than it did as a tiny contact sheet print (remember my circled-under eyes). You will be able to choose just the right business headshot from the blow-ups. Once you've made up your mind, invest in prints.

## Ordering Duplicates

Don't ask the photographer to make your prints. You'll need to order at least a hundred or more to start, and that would cost hundreds of dollars. Instead, take the headshot of your choice to a quality custom photo service for quantity reproduction. They'll do the work for much less.

Choose your custom photo lab with care, again using the recommendations of actors, agents, casting people, and your photographer. For a quality, professional look, order your pictures in mat finish with no borders. Stay away from glossy finish to avoid fingerprints. Have your name printed in an understated typeface in the lower right- or left-hand corner.

Some photo labs offer retouching services, but this is not always a good idea. Remember not to do anything that will alter the way you look in person. Any retouching must be invisible and very subtle.

## ✳ *Postcards*

The picture postcard is one of the most widely used promotional tools used by actors today. Actors send them everywhere and use them for several purposes, and for keeping in touch and for thank-you notes they are indispensible in the corporate world. The picture postcard has your photo printed on one side with a space for a brief message across the bottom. The other side is blank for an address and a more detailed note or message (see Figure 5.2).

Order your postcards from the same custom photo lab that prints your headshots. You can use the same photo you chose for your eight-by-ten or, better yet, use your second choice. Reproducing your second choice for the postcard is a little more expensive since it involves an additional negative at the photo lab. But it makes sense because it allows you to give everybody you meet a second look at you. The first time you meet an agent, casting director, or producer at an audition, you will give them your headshot. But when you follow up, the postcard will come into play; a fresh look on that card is an advantage.

Here's an idea. If you've chosen a smiling shot for your eight-by-ten, why not go for a serious one for your postcard? Or you could try the reverse.

When ordering headshots and postcards, purchase as many as you can afford. Good photo labs charge less for prints when purchased in volume, and if you plan to seriously attack this business, your supply of headshots and postcards will be depleted rapidly. Plan on ordering at least 100 of each, but if you have the resources, 250 of each will cost you less in the long run.

Headshots and postcards will help you find work only if they are used to their best advantage. We'll discuss when and where tzo send them in chapter 6.

## ✳ The Business Resume

As every experienced actor knows, you will need to paste or staple an eight-by-ten resume to the back of your headshot.

Linda Carole Pierce                              AEA SAG AFTRA

5.2   Linda Carole Pierce uses two headshots for her "composite" postcard. You can do the same. Notice how she lists her union affiliations on the postcard.

Many producers prefer pasting because the resume is less likely to become separated from the headshot with wear.

To state the obvious, your resume is important no matter what segment of the acting field you want to penetrate; but in the industrial arena, it's vital.

## The Generic Resume

The vast majority of actors today use a somewhat standardized format for their resumes that looks like an attempt to be all things to all people. I call it the generic resume because it contains listings for film, television, industrials, theater, and commercials as well as information on training and special skills.

# LINDA CAROLE PIERCE
### SAG - AFTRA - AEA

## FILM / TELEVISION

| | | |
|---|---|---|
| New Jack City | Day Player/Tenant | Warner Bros. |
| Penn & Teller Get Killed | Day Player/Nurse | Lorimar Productions |
| As The World Turns | U/ 5 | NBC |
| One Life To Live | U/ 5 | ABC |
| America's Most Wanted | Day Player | National Syndication |
| Jehovah's Witness | Principal/J.W. | PBS Documentary |
| Dumped On | Principal | ABC Pilot |

## OFF BROADWAY

| | | |
|---|---|---|
| One Tit, A Dyke & Gin | Gina | Sanford Meisner Theatre |
| Girlfriends | Melody | Riant Theatre |
| The Break | Peggy | Village Gate (One Act Festival) |
| Blessed Events | Gertrude | 29th Street Theatre |
| Waiting for Joyce Miller | Joyce Miller | RAPP Arts Theatre |
| A Wound in Time | Priestess | Third Step Theatre |
| Ira Aldridge Finalist | 1st Annual | Negro Ensemble Company |
| Creative Arts Team/C.A.T. | Aids Literacy | NYU Outreach |

## REGIONAL THEATRE

| | | |
|---|---|---|
| Shakespeare Repertory | Ophelia/Emilia | Walnut Street Theatre |
| Lysistrata | Lysistrata | Villanova University Theatre |
| Much Ado About Nothing | Ursula | Foundation Theatre |
| Little Victories | Joan of Arc | Daughter Productions |
| President's Daughter/ | | Daughter Productions & |
| President's Wife | Sally Hemmings | Bristol Riverside Theatre |
| An Evening With ... | Josephine Baker | Bushfire Theatre |
| Purlie Victorious | Lutie Belle | Walnut Street Theatre |
| Wedding Band | Lula | Theatre Centre |
| A Raisin in the Sun | Beneatha | Walnut Street Theatre |
| For Colored Girls ... | Lady in Purple | Shubert Theatre |
| Life Issues Drama | Various Roles | Plays For Living |

## COMMERCIALS ( conflict list upon request)

## CORPORATE/EDUCATIONAL VIDEOS & TRADE SHOWS (Principal)
Chase Manhattan Bank; IBM; Xerox; Memorial Sloan Kettering; Bell of PA; City of
Philadelphia Anti Drug Campaign; Conrail; C&P Telephone; Corp. for the Aged; First
PA Bank; Penn Mutual Insurance; SmithKline Beckman; SQUIBB; Sun Oil;
International Hair & Beauty Big Show Expo.

## TRAINING / SKILLS
| | |
|---|---|
| Temple University-School of Comm. & Theater | HB Studios - Francis Foster |
| RAPP Arts Theatre (Scene Study) - Jeff Cohen | Weist Barron School |

**Classroom Instruction:** Drama for Youth; Conflicts/Resolution Mediation
**Computers:** MAC/ IBM **Hobbies:** Horseback Riding; Biking; **Accents:** various

5.3 This solid generic resume has a decidedly theatrical focus
leading off with film and television. The heavy emphasis on theater is obviously important to this New York-based actress. Notice
that her industrial credits, which she labels CORPORATE/EDUCA-
TIONAL, are placed near the end of the resume.

Beginners flesh out their resumes with emphasis on training and theater, while experienced professionals load up the document with theatrical, film, television, and major theater credits while downplaying industrials and commercials (see Figure 5.3).

Although such a resume is very serviceable, particularly in New York City and Chicago where theater credits provide status, it may not give you an edge in the corporate environment, or any other segment of the market for that matter. Many experienced actors realize this and now tailor their resumes to attract more industry-specific attention. You should consider doing the same.

Beginners should start out with a nicely designed generic format. There are many books out there, including *Stay Home and Star,* that will help you put that first resume together. This resume will be compiled to show off your versatility and can be used to seek work in any area of the business. But for the following discussion, let's examine resumes tailored to the corporate world. These might lead to more work in that area for more experienced actors who already have several industrial credits.

## The Industrial-Specific Resume

When designing your resume for the corporate world, the idea is to make it coordinate with all your self-promotion to present a conservative, businesslike image. In other words, your resume should be cleanly designed with no cute theatrical touches.

Here's one approach to a corporate-specific resume. Use it if you want, but don't feel that it represents the only way to go. Be creative. Perhaps you have developed a specialty within the corporate television world you could incorporate into your own unique resume.

The corporate-specific resume runs close to the generic resume but puts extra weight on your industrial films cate-

**BOND FARLEY**
**SAG/AFTRA**
Tel: 123.456.7899

| 38 Blackstrap Rd. | Height: 6' | Hair: Br/Grey | Suit: 42r |
| Anywhere, USA 12345 | Weight: 180 | Eyes: Hazel | Shirt: 15 1/2-34 |

**INDUSTRIAL FILMS** ( On Camera Principal/Narrator - Partial Listing)

| I.B.M. | A. T. & T. | U. S. NAVY |
|---|---|---|
| UNITED AIRLINES | MILLER BREWING | N. E. TELEPHONE |
| ROCKWELL | TRAVELERS INS. | FILENES |
| BENDIX | HONEYWELL | HEWLETT PACKARD |
| HANOVER INS. | UNUM INS. | DIGITAL EQUIPMENT |
| DATA GENERAL | BOISE CASCADE | EDUCATIONAL TESTING |
| WHIRLPOOL | LIBERTY MUTUAL | INTERNATIONAL PAPER |
| WANG | POLAROID | GROSSMAN'S LUMBER |
| JOHN HANCOCK | BATH IRON WORKS | NATIONAL ASSN. REALTORS |
| PRUDENTIAL INS. | PITNEY BOWES | PROVIDENT MUTUAL |
| BLUE CROSS | HOOD SAILS | AETNA INS. |

**FILM**

| MERMAIDS... | Fred  (Principal) | Richard Benjamin, Dir. |
|---|---|---|
| THE DEFECTION OF | | |
| SIMAS KUDIRKA (MOW) | Sullivan  (Principal) | David Lowell Rich, Dir. |
| COMA... | Security Guard | Michael Chriton, Dir. |

**TELEVISION**

| AGAINST THE LAW... | Dr. Lupin (Featured) | Fox Television |
|---|---|---|
| MILLER'S COURT... | John (Lead) | Metromedia |
| ELI  &  THE WHALE... | Father (Co-Star) | WCVB-TV, Boston |
| BACKSTAGE... | Host (Weekly) | Maine Public TV |
| NEWS/SPORTS... | Anchor | WLBZ-TV, Maine |
| | | (NBC Affiliate) |

**COMMERCIALS:**     Conflicts available on request

**SPECIAL SKILLS:**     Sailing, Skiing, Public Speaking, Rock Climbing, Drive/Own car, U.S. Passport.

**EXTENSIVE EARPROMPTER EXPERIENCE / DEMOS AVAILABLE**

**5.4** An industry-specific resume of a New England-based regional actor targeting industrial films as his primary line of work.

gory through the number of entries and their placement (see Figure 5.4).

By putting your corporate credits at the top of the resume you immediately draw attention to them and show anyone who sees the resume that this segment of the business is your top priority. Industrial producers will like this At a glance, they can also see with whom you have worked.

Your list of clients is extremely important because psychologically each industrial listing is a subtle reference. Let's say you're auditioning for a spokesperson role for Aetna Insurance. You walk into the room and hand over your headshot and resume, called a *headsheet,* to the producer/director who's running the session. You shake hands, say hello, and wait for instructions.

What do you think the first thing that producer/director will do after looking at you? Look at your headsheet, that's what. And this person either will or will not be impressed on the weight of your industrials listing, which—in this close-to-generic format—should include a list of your industrial clients *and* note your proficiency with the earprompter, foreign languages, and business-specific tools such as computers. Remember to not list the earprompter if you are not completely proficient with it.

If this producer/director sees immediately that you have been a spokesperson for major corporations on a level with Aetna, your stature will rise. Your resume will have given you an edge over actors who have chosen to bury their corporate work deep within their resumes. It's that simple. Actors who choose this custom approach usually follow the "industrials" heading with legitimate film and television credits and, lastly, with commercials.

In general, actors will refer to the fact that they have appeared in commercials only with a header followed by the statement "Conflicts upon request." This makes sense for all resumes because once you appear in a television spot, producers will shy away from you if the company they represent competes with the product in your commercial. Even corporate producers won't touch you if they think their company's employees will watch you on commercial television selling the other guy. For this reason it is always better to keep specific commercial clients off your resume.

If you have not appeared in any commercials, do not include a commercial category on your resume.

# Additional Self-Promotional Tools

Everything you do in approaching corporate clients should be coordinated to make a statement—that you're a person of order and composure who understands the dynamics of the corporate environment.

— *Tersh Raybold*
*Corporate Producer*

*N*ow armed with a great business headshot, post-cards, and resume, it's time to ensure the rest of your promotional tools fall into line. Let's very briefly turn our attention again to your wardrobe and then move on to the other things you'll need to flesh out your business image.

## ✳ Wardrobe

It almost goes without saying that everyone you meet in the corporate environment will examine you carefully to see how they feel about you. You need to fit into their orderly expectations by always looking your best in business terms—well groomed and well dressed with appropriate accessories.

*100*

Too many actors forget about the importance of expectations by wrongly assuming that they will be forgiven their eccentricities because they are actors and therefore somehow immune from the rules that govern the rest of the world.

At the earliest opportunity, both women and men should assemble a business-oriented wardrobe of several outfits. Keep in mind the points raised in chapter 2 and in the discussion of headshots; this wardrobe should work for you whether you're on or off camera.

Of course, the right clothes will be costly, but if you start with the basics and build on that, it won't be long before you're ready for any eventuality.

My fundamental rule: When it comes to wardrobe and jewelry, basic is always better. Therefore, the first purchase for both men and women should be a conservatively cut, high-quality banker's gray suit with black shoes; a pastel blue, off-white, or gray shirt or blouse; and a red paisley tie or scarf with a muted design. Men should purchase over-the-calf socks. Women should wear flesh-toned hose of roughly their skin color in winter. A pale tint is acceptable in spring and summer. Ladies, remember that you *must* wear hose!

Your second outfit should consist of a camel blazer with brown slacks or skirt or a dark blue sportcoat with gray slacks or skirt. Avoid navy, charcoal, and black—they turn into dark blobs on video. All skirts should cover the knee. When you start adding outfits, go for a blue suit as your next selection and then move on to pinstripes.

These outfits will serve you well in almost all situations. I find that my plain gray suit with a blue button-down shirt and red tie is selected by directors over 80 percent of the time. The blazer comes into play whenever a director wants a slightly more casual look.

Stay away from *pure* black, white, or red (video hates red because it smears on the duplicate VHS cassettes) and tiny, busy patterns. Women, remember what I said about jewelry?

Keep it simple. Don't let your jewelry get in the way of the microphone or draw the eye.

What about white shirts? The automatic gain on video cameras will adjust for the brightness of the white collar by darkening the whole picture, turning the actor's face into a tanned splotch. In turn, the video technician will stop everything and ask the gaffer to relight to throw less glare on the shirt, which will then cause the producer to ask if you have a nonwhite shirt with you.

## ✳ *Printed Materials*

Your business image will also be enhanced when making direct contact with corporate video producers through personalized, custom-printed materials.

Business actors need to invest in a business card and a letterhead at the very least and should also consider mailing and demo tape labels as well. If money is a problem at first, go to one of those quick-print shops and order your materials in basic black type printed on a plain white inexpensive stock. You'll be surprised at how little you'll spend to look clean, straightforward, and professional. Do not select a generic logo that everyone else is using.

After you've started working in industrials, you should seek to upgrade your printed look by commissioning a *personalized* logo and go for quality paper stock so that your materials will look and feel better.

During the process of writing this book, I decided, for the second time in my career, to invest in a completely new print image. I hired a local freelance graphic artist to design a logo and supervise the printing of color-coordinated cards, a letterhead, postcards, and labels (see Figure 6.1).

In the business community we are judged, sometimes quite unfairly, on style over substance. Knowing that, it only makes sense that you shouldn't cut corners in matters of

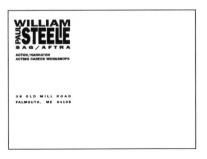

**6.1**    I use these print materials to present a coordinated business image on paper.

style. If you agree that you shouldn't purchase a poorly cut suit, why should you buy *any* image-enhancing item that is anything less than high quality? Poor style just doesn't make good business sense.

On the other hand, I do not mean you shouldn't seek out a bargain. When I buy a new suit, I always buy from the best stores in the off season. When I need a new print job done, I put it out to bid. It takes time and effort to get a good deal, but it's worth it to get quality, because *quality* is a key word.

For example, say a producer you've never heard of who works for an appealing company calls you and requests a headsheet and audio and video demo tapes. This may happen frequently once you get going in the business.

Remember, this person has never met you. Neither have any of the people to whom your promotional package will be presented. What will those people be looking for? Well, obviously, great acting and voice talent, as revealed by your demo tapes. But they'll also have questions about your professionalism. They'll want to know if you are efficient and easy to work with.

Since you're not there to tell them how wonderful you are, your promotional presentation will have to do the job for you. The personalized mailing label, the letterhead you write your brief message on, your quality headshot, a nicely printed resume, and the label-coordinated demo tapes become vitally important in selling you as someone who knows what he or she is doing and who means business.

## ✷ Demo Tapes

Business actors need audio and video demo tapes for a very simple reason: Most corporate projects nationwide are cast in-house, without the services of either casting or talent agencies.

Before going any further, let me stress that auditioning for industrials (see chapter 7) is still a very important way to get on-camera jobs. And in some cities, such as Los Angeles or New York City, it's the major way. But when you look at industrial casting nationally, auditions are most definitely secondary to demo tapes.

## Audio Demo Tapes

An audio demo tape should be your first priority, particularly if you feel you have the voice to compete for narrations, the category into which the vast majority of corporate work falls. Character actors and people with unusual voices will also need an audio demo. A unique voice, provided it's appealing, is always in demand in audio role-plays and narrations. If you speak any foreign languages fluently, you should put together a demo tape for each language.

In *Stay Home and Star* I spelled out a workable strategy to help beginning actors put together a voice demo that would serve until a new one could be made using produced work. My suggestion involved working with an established audio studio using copy they provide or that you track down to produce your first tape. I suggested that the first tape be comprehensive, including commercial as well as industrial reads.

That strategy is fine for an aspiring actor who wants to connect at all levels of the acting business, but once you have the resources to put together specialized tapes you should do so. Because most industrial producers are not interested in hearing commercial reads, it only makes sense to put together a tape that has been designed for the specific kinds of jobs you are seeking.

When putting your industrial audio demo together, there are a couple of things to keep in mind. First, keep it relatively short, about three to four minutes in length, and don't put anything of poor production quality on the tape.

When producers listen to audiotapes, they usually don't listen very long before deciding whether or not your voice is appropriate for a specific job. They probably won't listen for the full three or four minutes. If you are compiling a tape from work you've done, start the tape with the piece that delivers your best straight conversational corporate read that is not set to music. Then follow that with as much variety as you can in fifteen- to thirty-second segments to reach the desired length. It's important to put contrasting styles on the tape to show your range. Try to impress the listener—if you can—with big client names.

For reference, I have eleven pieces on my three-minute corporate audiotape with some straight conversational narration, narration set to music, hard sell, documentary style, and dialogue.

If you're just starting out and have no produced industrial voice work on hand, you should avail yourself of the services of a professional studio that routinely produces audiotapes for industrial producers. Professional help will not be cheap, but your tape should have a better chance of being competitive if it's professionally produced, assuming, of course, that you have a competitive voice.

Again, start the tape with a straight conversational read. This choice is very important. In about 90 percent of industrial narrations you're talking *to* people, not *at* them. You're not selling product. You're trying to relate to them as people.

Second, use cassette format. Nobody uses reel-to-reel anymore. Try to have your master recorded on digital audiotape (DAT) and carefully protect that tape from damage. From this DAT tape, make a working master from which you can make copies using home audio equipment.

If you plan to approach corporate voice work seriously you'll send out audio demo tapes as fast as your headsheet. So unless you want to go broke, you'll need to order blank cassettes in bulk and make copies at home. This means you'll need an inexpensive dual cassette deck.

Once you have your working master and your dual deck, you're ready to go. You'll be able to send out demo tapes for pennies a copy. That's right, pennies. Ask someone at a local recording studio where they buy their tape supplies. You'll probably receive the names of several vendors from whom you can request catalogs. You'll find that it's cheaper to buy your tapes in round lots of one hundred or more. And don't forget labels and boxes. Order the kind of labels designed for professional printing.

## Video Demo Tapes

Video demo tapes, of course, are a necessity for an on-camera spokesperson/narrator. They are not, however, absolutely essential for dramatic actors, because casting for dramatic roles is driven primarily by auditions. But a wise corporate actor will put together a video demo tape to take advantage of self-marketing opportunities as soon as it becomes practical to give casting directors a tool to use when you are unavailable to audition.

When does a video demo become practical? As soon as you have enough *produced* video samples of acceptable quality to show off your abilities.

As Nancy Doyle, a Boston casting director, puts it, "I don't think people should use demo reels unless they're excellent." She is, without question, correct. You should not automatically put everything you've done on a demo reel. You must be selective and choose only those pieces in which you are clearly featured and that have good production values. Don't just throw a tape together.

Obviously, you must obtain copies of your work from producers—which is sometimes difficult to accomplish. One way to ease the process is to make it your personal policy to request a copy of your work as a condition of your employment. If producers know up front that they are responsible for getting a copy of your work to you, you will find it much easier to actually get copies. And do not put off requesting copies of your work. Get on it right away, before the producer's attention turns away from you and on to another project.

There are two schools of thought on the video demo tape. One school holds that it should contain only industrial work. The other school believes that it should be comprehensive. In this case I opt for the comprehensive approach because there's much more than your voice involved here.

You will be judged, at least subconsciously, by the company you keep on your video demo reel. Producers will want not only to see how you look, move, and interpret copy, they'll also want to know who your clients are. So it helps to think of the demo tape as a video resume.

Keep in mind the suggestions made for your headsheet resume.

- *Where should I place my industrial samples?* At or near the top.

- *Which samples should I use?* The ones that show conversational narrative ability first if you are a spokesperson, followed by dramatic pieces interspersed with different styles of narration, including at least one voice-over segment.

- *What should I put after my industrial samples?* Film work if you have it, followed by commercials. Again, don't put anything on the tape that isn't well produced. Try to keep the tape under ten minutes in length.

Bob Boyd of Continuum Training Corporation offered some very good advice regarding video demos.

For you, a demo reel is a sales piece, so your performance and how you handle script and walk and talk at the same time is important. But you want people to see you in a glittering context. That's really important, because it tells me that you've worked in some really big budget stuff. Your demo reel should also tell me that you can use an earprompter or a teleprompter.

There's something else that's important, and that's to let me know who these video clips were made for. Don't just throw in a generic narration or role-play without at least including a character-generated company name. Subconsciously I'm going to say "Gee, she's worked for Aetna. She must be good."

There is no question that producers associate quality with quality, so choose samples of your work that are good television. If it's written poorly or looks inferior, don't use it. Even if you think a piece shows off your best performance and the lighting is bad, that production value might have a negative impact on the viewer, and you can't afford that.

Again, purchase your videotapes in bulk and in VHS format. They're available from the same suppliers of audiotapes you discovered when you did an audio demo and are much less expensive than buying them even at deeply discounted retail prices.

You also should consider used tapes. Ask around at video production houses, at television stations, and even at the corporate studios that know you. Some of these places may even give them to you. I'd recommend your getting fifty to a hundred tapes to start and begin recording your duplicates at home with rented equipment. You'll be able to churn out those video demo tapes for pennies a copy, too. Remember, once you've made your video demos, dress them up with custom-printed labels for a finished, professional look.

Armed with the promotional tools outlined above, it's time to get out there and do the real business of acting for business: looking for work.

# Looking for Work in Industrials

Direct marketing is best for narrators and spokespersons, even if they have an agent. For dramatic actors, it isn't unless they work as narrators and spokespersons, too.

— *Carol Nadell*
*Selective Casting*

*T*he process of looking for industrial acting work begins by understanding both how corporations and production houses seek out talent and how they prefer to be approached by actors. Once you know the rules, the mechanics of mapping out your job search create a very straight line.

Corporations in every region of the country seek out talent in a number of specific ways. When a production is being cast *in-house* by a producer or director who works for the company, familiarity usually rules. The producer/director's "corps" of actors (some producers call it their "stock" company) will be called into play unless that corps does not contain the specific type of performer required by the script or those in the corps who *are* right for the role have been overused or overexposed. Overexposure in industrials occurs when an actor has appeared in too many videos for the same client. At this point the search will broaden to include casting agencies, which are companies designed to find actors for producers.

When a production is being cast by an outside vendor such as a production house, the corps principal again takes center stage; but because budgets are usually higher when vendors are involved the casting agency may be called in at the outset.

These two realities should tell you something. If you want to work a lot, you must get into the actors corps of several producers, directors, and production houses. And you need to make sure that all of the casting agencies in your area call you in for auditions on a regular basis. Reaching such a level of exposure will take some doing.

## ✳ The Corps Concept

The corps concept is at the heart of the way every business does business. Think of it this way: The main thing that drives the selection of any business resource, whether it's a printer who puts together company brochures or a computer repair contractor, is time and reliability. Once a business locks on to a contractor who delivers a service in a timely manner with consistent quality and reliability, it's difficult for a competitor to shake that relationship.

When it comes to industrials, producers can't abide uncertainty, which is something they do everything they can to eliminate. If they have a budget for something that should be shot in three days but only one day in which to shoot, they do everything they can to remove any doubt about the production process in advance. If given the opportunity by the content of the script, producers will turn to actors they know and trust, people who have been proven efficient and reliable and with whom they have developed a comfortable working relationship. These people are the corps; they work for the same producers over and over again.

You should know that it is very difficult to break into a producer/director's corps of actors. Sometimes it seems as though it's impossible, but it's what you have to do to work—particularly if you are a narrator/spokesperson—because the vast majority of industrial work is done by corps members. Make it a point to always seek out even the smallest roles from producers who don't know you since they frequently try out a new talent in a minor role and then move them up if they come through on camera.

All of the industrial producers interviewed for this book report that they draw from a corps of fewer than ten actors—and usually only four or five—who fall into the narrator/spokesperson category. They also indicate that they have a larger corps of dramatic actors that tends to number in the teens. These producers said it is much easier for a dramatic actor to break through the corps barrier than it is for a narrator/spokesperson.

The breakthrough almost always occurs when the producer/director wants either a new face for a particular project or a person with special looks or physical abilites to meet script requirements. Where, then, does the producer/director begin to look for new talent?

If the project has the budget to warrant it, a casting session will be arranged through a casting agency. But in most cases budgets are restricted, and casting must be done in-house. This is when your self-marketing efforts are most likely to pay off. But how do you market yourself to corporations and casting agencies? As with everything else, in a very businesslike manner.

## ❋ Direct Marketing

### The International Television Association

The quickest way to make immediate contact with the producers of industrials is to join or get to know a member of the International Television Association (ITVA). The ITVA bills itself as "The Organization for Professional Video Communicators" and is the association of choice for video producers.

Joining ITVA is easy. All you do is write to them and request an application form.[1] When you receive it, send it back with your membership dues check. Every year you'll receive a complete membership directory that contains names and titles, addresses, and phone numbers of all members by chapter and by company. The directory is an invaluable resource and will save you days of digging through other directories.

The ITVA is broken into several regional chapters, one of which will be at least reasonably close to you and to which you will be assigned. This assignment will entitle you to attend your chapter's monthly meetings where you can meet producers and directors on a somewhat social level. Many successful industrial actors across the country belong to the ITVA, but all would agree that chapter meetings are not the place to aggressively market oneself. While it is appropriate to introduce yourself at meetings, don't sell. Meet people, but keep a low profile. After all, you're new!

Use the ITVA to build a prospect list of people whom you have met and who will remember you when you contact them on a business level. On the other hand don't forget to have business cards with you when you go to these events. Although you will not be handing them out unrequested, it's always good to have cards handy if anyone asks.

---

1. ITVA, 6311 N. O'Connor Rd., LB51, Irving, TX 75039. The telephone number is (214) 869-1112.

## Other Sources for Names

If the ITVA isn't for you or if you want additional names for your prospect list, consult your fellow actors. "What?" you say. "My fellow actors? Why would they help the competition?" This is a reasonable point, but since actors are by nature a supportive group, they *do* share contact names all the time.

Also try the yellow pages. Look up the general phone numbers of major companies in your area and call them. Ask for the audiovisual department, the media department, the television department, or whatever else seems relevant. Ask the department secretaries for the names of producers and add them to your list.

Finally, every time you audition for an industrial producer at a casting agency, write down that person's name and affiliation, and—even if you don't get a job—remember to follow up.

If you limit your name search to just these four avenues, you will soon develop a long list of prospects that will keep you busy for some time. And it will surely lead to even more names when you ask for referrals. Your final list should include the names of all the corporate, production house, and independent producers in your working area. This list could contain hundreds of names depending on where you live.

## Making Contact

Making personal contact with *everybody* on your list may be impossible; but by starting at the top and working steadily down, you should at least meet with some success if you use a reasonable, conservative approach.

Most producers indicate that they are receptive to a short, businesslike phone call for an initial contact. Some prefer the mail. Go with the majority here and use the phone, because if you can talk with someone before sending in your promotional information, you'll stand a better chance of having your materials reviewed. If a producer won't talk with you, accept that and *then* try to make contact through the mail.

The hard truth is that producers and directors are on a daily basis literally inundated by actors' promotional materials. They usually reserve a few file cabinet drawers to hold pictures and resumes and dedicate a shelf or two for demo tapes. After a while they become desensitized to the constant barrage of job-hungry actors who bug them for work.

But they do need actors and they know it, and good producers and directors keep an eye out for fresh faces and voices they can use. These are the producers who will talk to you when you call; they are the ones who will look at your materials. The others won't unless they have to. You might catch one of these at just the right time when they are looking specifically for someone out of their corps.

Start calling and don't be put off if several producers seem uninterested. Sooner or later you'll begin to hit the receptive ones.

When you call, you have two objectives. The first is to win a face-to-face meeting with the producer. The second is to let the producer know that you are mailing your materials and to subtly request that they be reviewed.

Getting a meeting may not be easy. Producers are busy, and they may have set up contact rules that insulate them from just the kind of meetings you want to arrange. But try anyway.

Once you have the person on the phone and have introduced yourself, you might phrase your request this way: "I know you're not familiar with my work, and I certainly would be happy to send you a headshot, resume, and demo reel, but would it be appropriate for me to come in for a brief meeting? Perhaps we could look at my tape together."

If the reply is yes, you're on your way. If it's not, follow up with something like this: "Well, would it then be OK to mail you my materials?" The answer to this question will almost always be yes, but ensuring that they *will* look at what you've sent in requires another question. "Great, I'll send them right away. By the way, I don't want to bug you, but may I call you in a week or so to be sure they arrived and to ask you what you think?"

Again, if you've gotten this far, you will probably receive an affirmative response. But if you are told not to call, don't. They'll call you if your materials spark interest.

Then mail your headsheet and voice demo and, if you have one, your video demo. Include a letter, preferably on your custom letterhead, thanking them for speaking with you on the phone and reminding them that you'll call in a week or so to check in—if they said that was appropriate.

Then wait a week and follow up with another call or, if a call is forbidden, your picture postcard containing a message.

> A week ago I sent you my headshot and resume, along with my demo tapes. I hope you've had a chance to review them. I would be happy to meet with you at your convenience and am always available to audition. Thank you for your consideration. Sincerely,

Be sure to include your address and phone number on the card and on all promotional materials you send.

You may have to phone more than once to determine whether your materials have been reviewed. Don't be bashful. Call twice or more or until it becomes obvious to you that you are being ignored. Then use the mail with that producer. If you follow this basic procedure, sooner or later you'll get some bites, providing you have a marketable look and talent to go with it.

Another way to make yourself known to production house producers is to simply drop in, ask the receptionist for the names of all the in-house producers, and ask if you may speak to one of them. You might get lucky. If that doesn't work, you can leave your promotional materials at the desk and request that they be put into the right hands.

A week later, call the receptionist to find out where your materials went and then ask to speak with that person. Do you get the idea? I thought so.

If you are awarded a face-to-face meeting, here's what to do:

- Arrive *on time.*
- Bring all of your promotional materials with you even if you've already sent them in—they may have been misplaced.
- Wear business attire that is suitable for television.
- Be extremely well groomed.
- Be assertive but not aggressive.
- Try to display your sense of humor and intelligence without being too obvious.
- Quietly sell yourself.

When asked to describe your experience, be forthright. Don't claim more experience than you actually have. Tell the producer what you've been working on and in the process indicate that you understand industrial television production while speaking indirectly about your work ethic. Remember, producers want to work with reliably efficient people who are easy to work with. Never forget these qualities.

If you sense that the meeting has gone well and that you have made a favorable impression, it's appropriate to ask the producer for the names of other producers whom you may contact. These additional names will be even easier to contact because you can approach them from the position of a recommendation. You can say, "When I met with Sarah Susan the other day, she suggested I give you a call," and so on. When you meet with that producer you can request even more names.

As soon as *one* of these producers gives you a job in which you perform well and prove that you are indeed reliable and easy to work with, you will find it much easier to obtain jobs and interviews. In the first place, you may have been added to that producer's corps. You also now have a work reference who will sing your praises and a fresh entry for your resume and demo tapes.

As you explore this avenue of meeting producers and building your own client list, remember to routinely update your promotional materials. Make sure your headshot always looks like you and don't let the pieces on your video demo tape get too old.

In time you will find that concentrated effort and persistence are key to your success. Never let rejection sway your purpose; keep an even keel and methodically reach for what you want.

Above all, never ever allow your prospects to sense that you are desperate. The moment a producer gets the idea that you *need* the work, you are finished. People buy from *confident* sales personnel, not from people who beg them to buy. That's just the way of the world. If you desperately need the work, you better find some work to do other than acting.

## ✳ Marketing Through Agencies

The above marketing strategies are closely aligned with the approach you must use when contacting talent and casting agencies, two businesses that have clearly different relationships with actors. Talent agencies represent talent. Casting agencies represent producers. The distinction is important to remember.

### Talent Agents

The way to approach talent agents differs from location to location, but their principal trade remains the same: They are there to represent you. *You* are their client. It is in their interest to find you work because they make money when you do.

But (and it's a big but) they will not try to find you work if they think you are not equal to the challenge. You have to be "right" for the work, marketable, and have the acting ability to be successful. Agents want to represent winners and will shun actors they perceive to be less than the best.

Just like producers, successful agents will surround themselves with a corps of reliable actors whom they trust, people they know will perform well and will not cause problems. If an agent is known for having a less-than-talented stable of actors, that agent's business days are numbered.

Business actors should also be aware that talent agents do not routinely represent actors who want to pursue industrials only. They prefer to work with actors who can be cast in the commercial and film markets because their commissions will be greater. They just don't make that much money from the industrials market. Many agents are also franchised by the actors' unions and are not permitted to represent nonunion actors.

Knowing this, you have to ask first whether or not you need an agent. Again, where you live will have a great deal to do with the way you answer this question.

## Big-City Agents

For example, if you live in New York City or Los Angeles and want a comprehensive acting career, agents are essential because casting agencies work through them to find actors. Even if you want to do industrials only—and the great majority of you *won't* want to limit your acting horizons—you will need an agent in these cities unless you are a spokesperson/narrator or nonunion, although casting agencies will call nonunion actors directly in New York and Los Angeles.

Big-city agents find actors through referrals (usually by their signed clients, who are actors they represent on an exclusive basis), showcases, scene nights, and plays. They also find actors through headshots and resumes.

The typical procedure for contact is simple. You send the agent your headsheet. Do not call. If the agent thinks it's a good picture and that you're a good type and in a needed age range, you will be called in for an interview and perhaps be asked to read. If the interview goes well, the agent will then start to work with you by sending you on a few auditions.

These big-city agents will send you out on auditions for commercials—and maybe even films, television series, and soap operas if they represent actors for the theatrical markets and if they think you're right—as well as industrials. If the feedback is good—if you start booking jobs right away or at least get called back regularly—then they may consider signing you to an exclusive contract.

Whether or not you should be represented by one agent in a large city is really a matter of preference. Many successful actors choose to freelance and work with several agents. Others prefer the security of being signed. When you reach the point where you are asked to sign, you'll have to make a decision based on the merits of both ways of doing business.

Finding agents in any city is easy: Use the yellow pages. If you're a union member, ask the union for a list of franchised agents or ask other actors. You'll find the agents very quickly.

## Smaller-City Agents

Outside major cities, talent agents are frequently modeling agents as well, so you may find them under the modeling agencies listing in the yellow pages.

Once you know who and where they are, making contact is usually a snap. Unlike their big-city counterparts, these folks are most often receptive to phone calls. Call them up, say that you are a new actor in town, and request an appointment. You might get lucky and be called in right away. If not, you'll at least receive instructions on what to do in the way of future contacts and probably be asked to mail in your headshot and resume.

Most smaller-city agents are not union affiliated, so you do not need to be a union member to be represented by them. In fact, if you plan to work as a small-city or regional actor, it may be in your best interest not to join a union at all, particularly if you want to focus on industrials. Most corporations use nonunion talent—and prefer it for financial reasons—even in large cities.

Small-city agents function in pretty much the same way as big-city agents: They send you out on auditions, usually at casting agencies, but they'll also try to get you work in print.[2]

## Casting Agencies

Casting agents do not represent you. Their clients are the producers who need actors for their videos and films. They owe you no loyalty, but all of the casting people interviewed for this book say they work from a corps, although their corps are usually much larger than those of typical producers.

Since casting agents work for producers, you must impress them in the same manner you have to impress everyone else. In addition, you have to consistently audition well in order to be on their list of actors who audition on a regular basis.

A bad audition makes casting agents look bad to their clients—producers. A clunky audition really makes a casting agent squirm. Too many clunkers in a casting session and the agent will not get called back.

Put casting agencies right under producers on your contact priority list. They are people you need, the ones who can get you jobs and provide names for your direct marketing efforts.

Now I'll turn to the single most important part of the industrials work-search process: auditioning.

---

2. See *Stay Home and Star,* Chapter 7, pages 115–128 for information on how to find work in the commercial and corporate print markets.

# The Industrial
# Audition

Often, the key to a corporate audition is making difficult
technical language seem simple and human.

— *Michael Lemon*
*Casting Director*

Auditioning well is a key to getting jobs in industrials, just as it is in all the other areas of acting. You must
walk in with an air of believable confidence and make an internal connection with the character. You must also read
well technically and make eye contact with the camera. You
must reveal that you can walk and talk at the same time.
Sound familiar?

It probably does to experienced actors who have auditioned for industrials, commercials, and films. It no doubt
rings a bell with inexperienced folks, too, who have read
some of the great books available on the subject of auditioning— books that deal with technique and psychology.

But the subject of auditioning *specifically* for industrials
needs your further attention because the rules that apply to
the other acting areas do not always apply here.

In the commercial audition you deal with minimal copy—even a sixty-second spokesperson read isn't much when compared to industrial narrative auditions. Your energy level for commercials is frequently required to be off the charts, and the characters you play are snapshots. You must find a way to flesh them out that is not always found in the copy. Commercial auditions are tough, but your look and voice quality are often more important than your ability to read well. Commercial directors figure that they ought to be able to get at least one good take out of a hundred from a person of normal intelligence.

In a theatrical film audition you're reading cold in front of people, with minimal time to prepare (but not *without* preparation). Only occasionally do you find a video camera at a film audition.

Here you are trying to find yourself in and make a personal connection with the character. You have to work from yourself. But, as is true with all human beings, your dramatic character is not perfect. Your character does not enunciate perfectly and neither should you. In fact, there's a very valid school of thought supporting less perfect theatrical film readings for longer roles. If it's one or two lines, read smoothly and clearly. If it goes beyond that, start to break it up with natural hesitations coming out of your honest connection with the character and your reaction to the stimuli you receive from your reading partner.

In an industrial audition, some of the above will apply, too. Your look and voice are important, and you must read believably. But since industrial roles are relegated primarily to spokesperson/narrators and corporate news anchors who impart large amounts of information and to dramatic characters who are written as either positive or negative role models, performance parameters are wider than those associated with commercial characters and narrower than those associated with film.

*All* auditions require a confident, enthusiastic attitude;

an ability to find humor, if there is any, in the situation; comfortable and appropriate physical involvement; maximum eye contact with the camera or person with whom you are reading; and the flexibility to take direction.

With the above in mind, I'll discuss the industrial audition and start with on-camera auditions.

## ✳ On-Camera Auditions

### Spokesperson/Narrator Auditions

For the purpose of this discussion let's put you in a typical industrial audition situation. You're trying out for an on-camera narrator who's explaining new computer software advancements to company employees—the national sales force—in a twenty-minute video. The industrial will be shot in a studio and will feature you in an office setting in which you manipulate a computer keyboard and talk to the camera. At least once in the narration you'll get up from your chair and walk around and lean on the desk while narrating.

When you arrive at the casting agency you already know most of the requirements. When you got the call, it was all explained. But you haven't yet seen the script. Armed with at least this sketch of what the job will entail, you wear a basic gray business suit as wardrobe, correctly deciding that you should look like one of the salespeople you'll address, someone with whom they will easily identify.

As you enter the waiting room, the first thing you do is sign in. You then receive a copy of the audition script with your lines highlighted. If it's your first time you probably say to yourself, "Whew! That's a lot of copy," because there is at least a couple of minutes there, probably more. What do you do now?

Try to ignore the other actors who hover nervously about. You don't want to catch their tension. Besides, you have work to do. You don't want to go into the audition room and read cold, do you? This is technical copy after all, and no matter how much you've practiced at home or how smoothly you've trained yourself to read, you still need to make some sense of it. You need to learn where the buzz-words are and where you should place emphasis. In the limited time you have, you also need to become as familiar as possible with the copy to help with eye contact.

Wisely, you study the script for a while by reading it through silently at least twice and underlining words—usually adjectives and adverbs—you determine need to be emphasized. You'll double underline the really important words. Then you try to get in a corner of the room or, better yet, out in the hall to read aloud to see how the script feels and to find any articulation traps the writer has inadvertently included. Reading aloud is important. Many industrial video writers are more adept at writing for technical clarity than they are at writing for the spoken word, and you have to make them look good by humanizing all that tech-talk. Sooner or later, probably within ten or fifteen minutes, your name is called and you enter the audition room. It's show time! Now what?

You walk in and show your confident self, that's what. When you're introduced to the producer/director, and perhaps even the producer/director's corporate client, you want to come across as an intelligent, easy-to-like, and real person. You want to somehow convey that very important impression that you're pleasant to work with. You do this, if given even the slightest opportunity, by displaying your sense of humor. But don't force anything and be relaxed and engaging. If the vibrations in the room are negative, as they so frequently are, don't fall into the trap of joining in. They've probably had a long day, so keep everything you do friendly, businesslike, and focused. Hand in your headsheet, shake hands if you can, and let the casting director tell you where to stand.

At this point the producer/director probably takes over by telling you what you already know. The information the casting director gave you when you got the audition call is repeated. Listen politely and listen for any facts that might clarify your interpretation of what you are about to read. You're then asked to state (or in film talk *slate*) your name and read after initial direction has been given.

*Forget about the people in the room and concentrate on the camera as the person with whom you are speaking.* Remembering your actual audience is essential. It's how you look on camera that's important, not how you look live.

Slating your name in a straightforward, pleasant manner is very important as well. Try something like, "Hi. I'm Bill Steele" with a warm—but not too big—smile, as you look directly into the camera. No histrionics here!

As you read (and *do* read; don't try to memorize the copy on the spot) the technical copy that you've been given, make as much direct communication with the camera lens as you possibly can without disrupting the *conversational* flow of the words. *Look* at that camera as if to say, "This is me. I'm an intelligent person. I'm talking to you, and we both understand what I'm saying and how important it is."

And while you're doing that, you try to find and project the humor that's inherent in the copy. That shows off your intelligence more than anything else and reveals that you're a relaxed, approachable, regular person to whom an audience will want to listen. Even if the copy is really cut and dried you should bring at least a little smile to it and warm it up. Humanizing the text should help you get the job.

After the first read-through, you may be asked to read again with closer direction. In this case, the person directing you is trying to determine if you can take direction, so *pay attention!* Try to the best of your ability to give what the director asked for, even if it doesn't feel right, and try to continue the positive energy flow established in your first read-through. After all, you wouldn't be asked to read a second time if your first reading didn't spark interest.

After this second reading you will be dismissed. Try to leave the room with the same businesslike confidence with which you entered by saying something like, "Thanks. Nice to meet you all." And stride for the door. Once back in the waiting room, don't linger. Just grab your things and leave. Hanging around won't help your cause, and it won't reinforce your business image either. Schmoozing in the reception room will be remembered by the annoyed casting agent.

Almost all spokesperson/narrator auditions relate to the above scenario. Of course, every audition *will* be different. Sometimes only the casting director will be in attendance, sometimes half a dozen corporate bigwigs. Sometimes there will be very little copy, sometimes pages and pages of it. Sometimes you'll be asked to be upbeat, sometimes deadly serious. You get the idea.

The important things to remember are:

- Dress appropriately.
- Prepare in the waiting room.
- Greet your auditioners personably.
- Look at the camera as a person as you read.
- Follow direction.
- Stay relaxed.

If you can do all these things, and you have appropriate looks and a marketable voice, you'll probably work all the time.

## Role-Playing Auditions

Now let's look at two role-playing scenarios. For the first one you've been called in to play the role of an executive in a meeting with an older employee who's teaching you the ropes.

When you arrive at the casting agency you again sign in and are given a script. This time you're also given a partner.

Right away the two of you should get down to business. You're reading a three-page scene and it needs a little analysis before you can humanize it. What's the problem in the scene? What does your character need to learn? What's your attitude going into the scene? How should you react to what you're being taught? Are you receptive or put off? Talk through these questions and those of your acting partner after an initial read-through.

If there do not seem to be answers to your questions, make some up; you need to audition with a character in hand and not a colorless person who spouts shop talk. Then you read through the scene a few times more until you're called in to do it for real.

When you go into the audition room, you shake hands with your auditioners, hand in your headsheet, and wait for direction. Again, the director of the audition, even if it's only the casting director, gives you a brief character sketch and you read the scene.

For this type of reading, forget about the camera and *listen to and feed off of your partner*. Working from within yourself, react to the stimuli given to you by your partner, even if it's not very much. *But do not overact or overreact*. Keep everything very small and very slice of life; go for ultra realism. Think *filmatic* style.

As you read through your scene for the first time, don't reword the script. Aim for as spontaneous a delivery as possible while making *maximum eye contact* with your partner.

Hold the script high enough so all you need to do is glance with your eyes—not your head—to find your lines, and low enough to reveal your full face and neck to the camera. You want to be able to look at your partner for as long as you can while your partner is speaking, only glancing at your script for your replies. Now is when all that at-home reading aloud really pays off.

Holding your script in this position also lets you see everything your partner does in terms of physical nuances and facial expressions, giving you something real to respond to in terms of interpersonal communication. It also helps you keep the pace of the scene moving along naturally, rather than haltingly as you search awkwardly for your lines.

After your initial reading, you'll be given specific direction based upon your first performance because you've performed well. Listen and try to deliver.

Your second role-playing audition is improvisational. This time you are the head honcho getting a sales pitch from two aggressive salespeople who are trying to get you to sign a contract for a major computer sale. Wear your dark blue suit, which gives you more authority than does your gray one. You arrive at the meeting in a mood to negotiate your best deal. The other players are already there, primed to get you to sign on the dotted line.

Your fortunes, in terms of whether or not you will be cast, depend largely on how you demonstrate power, not on how well you can invent dialogue. Remember, you're auditioning for a corporate CEO, not a playwright.

While in the waiting room you again practice with your partners, who are pressing you to buy. Ask pertinent questions and let them do most of the talking. People in power listen a lot.

When you go into the room, follow through on this theme. Ask questions, let them run on, sit back in your chair, and subtly relax. Try to give the impression that you control the situation.

Don't be afraid to interrupt their chatter, somewhat forcefully if you have to. This just plays into your role.

You're each given direction for a second run-through because your initial performance was good enough to warrant a second look. Again, you try to retain your air of power as you follow the directions.

The above role-playing scenarios are very typical, but there are some other things to keep in mind in an audition in which you and your partners are on the same business level. Here you still need to play the scene for power, and it will help you to think of the encounter as something of a game in which you will try to "score" subtle points.

Even though the scene will probably have been written simply to get information across to the viewer, you will humanize your character if you subtly celebrate your wins and react to your losses. You will also make the scene more interesting.

## ✳ News Anchor Auditions

Now let's put you in a different kind of spokesperson audition. This time you're shooting for the role of a news anchor.

Wear your dark blue suit. This time you are a true authority figure and a particularly trustworthy one. You are delivering news to the listener, and you must do everything you can to ensure that the listener accepts your information as gospel.

Your auditioners are looking for a couple of specific performance values from you: the ability to be newsy without losing credibility, and the skill to read from a script in your hand without looking at it very much. All contact is, of course, with the camera.

This kind of audition is very closely associated with the spokesperson/narrator audition. You need to be just as personable but with a slightly newsy tone. However, don't make the same mistake so many small-town news anchors do by editorializing. Just pass on the information in an up-beat, friendly manner without seeming to make value judg-ments.

The above audition scenarios apply for both men and women, but women should consider what Nancy Doyle of Boston's *Outcasting* says about playing executives.

> I've talked to a number of directors about this and they're *always* talking about female corporate execu-tives, women playing power. How do you work with a businesswoman in a really powerful position and have her be really strong without being bitchy? It comes more from relaxation and *knowing* that you have the power than *playing* that you have power. It's a very im-portant fine line that women have to find.

## ✳ Voice-Over Auditions

Auditions for voice-over work occur infrequently. When a voice is needed, demo tapes will be reviewed. So if you want to do industrial voice work, you need a good audio demo tape placed where it will do you some good—in the hands of producers, directors, casting agencies, and agents.

When auditions *are* held for voice-over work you'll sim-ply read the material into a microphone, but it will help if you are relaxed enough to take direction and make a per-sonal connection with the material. Of course, you must also maintain the same businesslike-yet-approachable attitude you carry into on-camera auditions.

Obviously, your voice quality and ability to interpret copy will be the keys to whether or not you audition success-fully for voice work. Still, it won't hurt to dress appropriately for an audio audition and wear business attire that's right for the camera. Why? The producer for whom you audition undoubtedly works with on-camera actors as well. Your voice-over audition just might land you an on-camera job some time later.

## ✳ Common Audition Mistakes

All of us who ply the business acting trade make mistakes in our job search efforts, particularly in auditions. At one audition we are completely on top of things, and the next time we seem to fall apart. We all want to be consistent in the audition process with the capacity to do the job well and always remain in complete control.

Experience, of course, does help in this quest for perfection. We learn from our successes, and we learn even more from our failures.

The following list of common audition mistakes is included here to save you time and pain. Learn from them.

### Showing up late

Starting with the obvious, the most common mistake relates to simple punctuality. In fact, you're better off showing up early so you'll have time to prepare. Actors who arrive right on the button run the risk of being ushered into the audition room at once. It happens all the time, but don't let it happen to you. You need time to get familiar with the copy and to become focused.

### Wearing the wrong clothes

Remember, this is business. Dress for business *and* for the camera. If you're unsure about what to wear, ask your agent or the casting director in advance. And have your wardrobe together. You want to look as "put together" and tidy as do people in a business environment. The impression you make when you walk through that door is all-important.

### Forgetting that the audition begins the moment you walk through the door

When you walk in, meet the client, and hand them a picture, you must be absolutely present and yourself. Clients need to see this "real" you if they haven't worked with you before. It won't help if you walk into that room already "in character." As Mike Lemon of Mike Lemon Casting in Philadelphia puts it, "Save the performance for when the camera starts rolling and forget the shtick."

### Wearing heavy make-up

Women should only use subtle street make-up. Men should only use translucent powder for excessive shine or to cover acne, but otherwise forget make-up.

### Walking in feeling that "this isn't for me"

Actors who go into an industrials audition thinking negatively about themselves or whether they are right for the role are usually dead in the water even before they start. They try to adjust with something that is less than genuine. The simple truth is that you can't always know what you're right or wrong for, so think positively. Work from yourself. Use your humor and intelligence.

### Asking too many questions

Actors who think they are going to gain an advantage with the client by asking lots of questions before they've even tried the copy run the risk of appearing too anxious. If the material is truly unclear, it's fine to ask a question, but questions that are asked to cozy up to a client are transparent.

### Working with glasses

Anyone who walks in wearing glasses as a prop—even though they don't wear glasses in life—is asking for trouble. It's a glaring indication that an actor is not in the moment.

### Using unnatural gestures or movement

If it's not a natural, integrated gesture or movement, forget it. Let gestures and movement come from the moment, from your involvement in the scene. If nothing happens during your first reading, so be it. At least it won't be phony. The second time through, if the director suggests an action, run with it.

### Beating yourself up if something doesn't go right during the audition

If you make a mistake, just keep going without reacting to it. If you do react by apologizing or, even worse, by stopping and asking to start again, you'll only draw attention to the fact that you're having problems, which is self-defeating.

### Giving up on your acting partner

If you are playing a scene with somebody who is not doing well or whose work is dragging the scene down, don't point out in the scene that it's her or his problem. Try to work with that person as best you can and use what you get. Try to help. Make adjustments. There is no other way to deal with this situation properly. If you try to make the best of it, maybe you'll be called in later to read with another person.

### Talking too much during an improv

If you try to dominate an improvisation by showing off how clever you are in the dialogue-writing department, you'll lose. Real conversation is give and take. Be fair. Give your fellow actors a chance to speak, too. And remember the rule of power: Sometimes less is more.

### Memorizing the copy

Don't memorize for auditions. Become as familiar with the copy as possible. If you feel you must memorize something, memorize the role, not the specific words. Your ability to work from yourself and make connections with the character is what's important here, not your ability to memorize. Use the script.

### Using the earprompter

Many producers will want to know if you are proficient with the earprompter, but the audition is not the place to use it unless your are so adept with the device that you can alter pace, energy, and interpretation *without* rerecording, which is almost impossible. In fact, it is impossible if the director wants you to significantly slow it down.

### Forgetting your headshot

Don't forget your headshot. It's unprofessional.


Certainly you will make other mistakes, but managing to avoid those listed here will go a long way in helping you to audition successfully.

# Working in Industrials

Your job as an actor is to figure out what they want in an audition so you can get hired, and then do what they want when you're on the set.

— *Cynthia Barnett*
*Business Actor*

I want a professional person who's going to give me a good day's work, who understands what that means in a corporate — as opposed to a broadcast or film—context.

— *Bob Boyd*
*Independent Producer*

*N*ow that you've prepared yourself, learned how business makes films and videos, and pried the casting door wide open through your auditioning efforts, you're ready to get to work, show up on that set, and knock them dead. Right? Well, not quite. You'll want to consider a few important things about the work environment before you get there.

## ✳ *Expectations*

Bob Boyd's comment above makes a lot of sense if you want to become a regular in the ranks of industrial acting. The word *professional,* as it is associated with actors, has a decidedly businesslike spin in the mind of industrial producers.

To them, the word does not mean that you are a person of great talent, although that definition may tangentially apply. *Professional* has more to do with work ethic than whether or not you're good at what you do. And it has nothing to do with stardom.

You will be judged on the quality of your performance, but you will also be assessed on your approach to your work, how you get along with other people, and whether or not you fit into the business environment. Ask any producer of industrials what's most important in an actor, and you may be surprised where the talent category falls.

Considering the wealth of talent available to producers today, acting ability is rarely the deciding factor as to whether an individual will be hired regularly. The actor's reputation is what counts. If your reputation is that you are difficult to work with, they'll find another talented actor. Actors deemed easy to work with will get the call over troublesome actors even though they may be perceived as more talented.

Tersh Raybold, formerly a producer at Whirlpool in Benton Harbor, Michigan, and now an independent producer operating in San Diego, puts it this way:

> Actors need to remember that in a corporation most of the producers work with big egos all the time and the last thing they want to do is pay someone several hundred dollars a day to give them a hard time. They can get that from their immediate boss or their other clients. So in many situations you may see people who

may not be the best actors, but because they're very friendly and very easy to work with, people will hire them again and again. These people also know how to act businesslike.

When asked what "acting businesslike" meant, Raybold replied:

> You're being paid to represent the company, so while you're there "act" like a business person. If you're being paid for a full day and a producer asks you to sit in a greenroom or office or somewhere and entertain yourself for a couple of hours do so without being a pest. Don't move around getting in people's way. Don't talk with people who are working. Don't fiddle with the equipment. Remember, everyone else is trying to do a job and get it over with as quickly as possible without sacrificing quality. Don't do anything to hinder that.

## Their Expectations of You

With all this in mind, you should know what industrial producers expect from the actors they hire so you can deliver it from day one. Let's start with what Bob Boyd means by "a good day's work."

What Boyd is really referring to has a lot to do with an actor's work ethic. Business people, at least the ones who commission videos and hire actors, are the kind of folks who put in long days. They're on salary and they rarely watch the clock. They stay on the job until whatever they're working on has been completed. And they frequently take their work home.

It's important for the corporate actor to understand that *they expect no less of you*. While there are certainly many business people who are impressed with the celebrity status of the actors they hire, most are not. Actors are viewed as contractors and are expected to give good value.

In the simplest of terms, this means that actors are expected to show up on time, be prepared, and get the work done—giving 100 percent 100 percent of the time—just like other employees who value their job.

Taken in this context, a good day's work means that you should expect to work at least eight hours for your day's pay with the same breaks everybody else gets. Having to leave early is totally unacceptable. You should also expect not to be put on a pedestal. On the industrial set you're not a star, but you are an important member of a production team. So you shouldn't expect to be treated with indifference, either.

If you are a member of an actors' union working under a union contract, your working conditions will be clearly spelled out, and it will be incumbent upon the producer to see that they are followed, but as Raybold says, "It's not fair of you to expect producers and directors to treat you like an artist. You're really just another worker to them who has a job to do." So be happy with what you get. This attitude is one of the things that will make producers see you as easy to work with.

Another important quality will be your ability to deal with the stress and strain of the entire day in a positive manner. Actors who complain about adverse working conditions are rarely asked back, even when they're right. So be nice, work cooperatively, and be flexible. Unpleasant people are the untouchables of the business of acting for business.

There are some other things you need to consider on any job.

### Be prepared

Industrial producers expect you to arrive on the set having read or memorized the script, whichever is required. If it's a role-play, memorize it as discussed in chapter 2. If your performance is prompted, you should at the very least be highly familiar with the script before you arrive on location. Obviously, all this means that you must receive the script in advance. Always request a copy at the time of booking to help ensure your having the script in your hands *before* you arrive at the shoot.

Budget factors dictate that you will rarely enjoy the luxury of rehearsal. Rehearse on your own to help ensure that the day, at least that your end of the day, will proceed smoothly. One way you can demonstrate the fact that you've studied the material in advance is to ask questions—but not too many!

If you make mistakes like coming in cold, not reading the script, or having no idea who your audience is, it will show. Take an interest in the material and demonstrate that interest. Producers expect to work with actors who are involved in their jobs. Lack of interest will come as a negative surprise.

You also should arrive with proper wardrobe and make-up for the job. This, too, is part of your expected preparation. Show up with as many clothing alternatives as you can muster and be prepared to do your own make-up. Producers like working with actors who can do their own make-up because it saves them money.

### Don't let your personal problems show on the job

Keep them to yourself. If you have a cold, try not to let it show. And don't dwell on it. Remember, the show must go on. Try always to create the impression that you enjoy working with everyone on the production team.

### Don't abuse your relationship with the director

The director is your immediate superior and expects you to take direction. Unlike the stage or theatrical film director who may give actors lots of interpretive latitude, industrial directors take a much more businesslike approach. Industrial directors expect actors to pay close attention to direction and to try to follow through without lots of questions. I don't mean to say that some questioning for clarification is inappropriate, but generally speaking the expectation is that you will "do what you're told."

Bob Feldman, an independent producer, has an important point to make on this subject.

> Sometimes I'll ask an actor to do another take without explanation. I just expect the actor to do it again and not make a big deal of it, not get mad at me because I don't explain in detail why I want something. I don't have to tell the actor anything! I just want it done again. It could be anything—a technical problem. So just do it. It's OK to ask, "Anything different?" But generally just do it again until the director is happy.

Of course, if you've worked with a director before and a relationship of trust has been established, then an atmosphere of shared contribution may work. Once you've been added to a director's corps, your suggestions for shot angle, movement, prop manipulation, and so on may be welcomed. But even then you shouldn't go too far.

Even if it's obvious that the director is not that well prepared and that your suggestions could save everyone time and improve the quality of the project, it might still be best to keep your ideas to yourself. The last thing you want to do is run the risk of making an insecure director feel threatened, particularly if a client is around.

Your relationship with any director should always be relaxed and positive, but admittedly that's not always possible. Some directors—very few in my experience—are unpleasant to work for. They may be overbearing, condescending, harshly critical, insensitive, obnoxiously egotistical, or whatever. But you don't have to be. When you run into directors who act like they are your worst enemy, you can either object in a professional manner or put on a pleasant face, keep your lips sealed, and do your job.

If you take the first approach by choosing to object, try not to let your anger get out of hand. Try to salvage the situation by objecting in a businesslike manner. Ask the director to speak with you privately and then state your case. Who knows, maybe that person is just having a bad day, and your ability to put up with it professionally rather than emotionally may land you another job. On the other hand, you don't *have* to work for this person again. It's your choice if you are offered a second job. So make sure you have a choice to make—you may need the work.

Web Lithgow of Commonwealth Films in Boston sheds some interesting light on this subject: "*Proper* direction helps the actor to look better on the screen. It is a *service* to the actor in the interests of making the performance, the scene, and the film more effective." He adds, "Acting is a tough and sometimes tedious job. The actor is as exposed to failure in public as a baseball player. I figure an actor doesn't need extra stress. So I go out of my way to avoid embarassing an actor on the set. In my view, an actor has the right to object if a director—either negligently or deliberately—gives direction in a manner calculated to demean or belittle."

In the final analysis the director is there to make the whole program look good, and that includes you. For that to happen you must learn to take direction, even if that means accepting the fact that you need it. But you do not have to accept humiliation.

### Don't horse around

It's fine to break tension with a joke or two, but constant kidding around will disrupt the shoot, confuse the working environment, and simply make it hard for your coworkers to hear or even think. There's no question that shooting an industrial video can be enjoyable with a crew that likes to have a good time. But there's a time to play and a time to work. You'll need to develop a sixth sense to catch the clues that the director is ready to get down to business.

### Don't leave the set

Ask!

### Don't be disruptive in the corporate culture

Lots of corporate videos are now shot on location at job sites where regular employees will be working or trying to work around you. Be sensitive to their needs. Do not display distracting laughter or boisterous behavior. Respect the work environment and try to stay out of the way. Remember, "act" businesslike!

### Don't forget the client

There is often a client on the set, and you should know who that person is and be aware of what they say about the script; but you should not let the client become your director. You can make a client either nervous or very relaxed and comfortable by the way you communicate about the script and what you are doing. Remember the script is very important to the client. Every word in it has been lovingly crafted and probably decided upon by committee. So treat it with the utmost respect, even if it's poorly written.

### Don't act self-important

You might get away with egotistical behavior on theatrical, television, and film sets, but not here. Industrial video is about as far away from a broadcasting/film culture as you can get. Remember, it's a lot of blue suits, red ties, lace-up shoes, and very serious people.

If you remember to avoid all of the above and simply get the job done as professionally and pleasantly as your talents and personality allow, you will build success in industrials.

## Working With Nonprofessional In-House Talent

There is one final expectation industrial producers have of professional actors that needs discussion here: *the capacity to work well alongside nonprofessional in-house talent.*

Every now and then a corporate presentation will feature a professional actor as spokesperson or interviewer working in a "team" environment with a corporate executive or two. This situation can spell trouble for the actor who is insensitive to the needs of nonprofessional performers; *you* are expected to control the situation, not the other person.

Most of the time the in-house talent will be interviewed, at worst in a scripted interview, and it will probably be a vice president, director, or even the president of the company. So think about what this person faces. Maybe the person understands television and is slick, but the chances are he or she is a Type A personality who has been taken from a normal realm of responsibility, which is usually total control and real power within the company, and thrust into a position where *the people who work below* have control over him or her by definition. The simple truth is that if this person of power does not become adjusted to this reversal of authority, a poor program usually results.

But how do you counteract the negative energy put forth by a person with security and power—a person who probably has immense drive and ego—who's been plopped into a situation lacking security and power? Well, with some of these folks you might run into a stone wall, but for most a simple buddy system is the best approach.

You must, through a calm, mature, and positive attitude, create an atmosphere of teamwork. A "don't worry, we'll get through this together and we'll both look great" view of things. Your conscious effort to repeatedly offer positive reassurance will be a major factor in whether or not you are successful in this effort. You'll need to let executives know you respect them, tell them what a great job they're doing, and take a genuine interest in what they say in the interview. These tactics are of utmost importance.

The executives must feel that they are having a real conversation in order to get past ego problems and relax. Even if the interview is scripted. For you, that means maximum eye contact with the executive, very relaxed body language, and a very genuine, unself-conscious demeanor. To get the person to forget the lights and really engage in a conversation, you must be a totally believable partner.

A trick many directors use to relax nervous executives is to get through a take and tell the executive that it was a winner. Then they request another take or so for insurance. You are expected to help in this process by reassuring the executive that, because a winner is already in the can, everyone may now relax through the insurance takes.

Actors who have a habit of saying, "Why do we need another take?" or, "What was wrong with that?" when another take is suggested are working against the director and against making the executive look good.

Sometimes, no matter what you do, executives just won't respond because they are threatened by your ability and are worried that they will be overshadowed by your performance. When this occurs, all you can do is maintain your positive, friendly attitude and let the director deal with the problem. Remember whose house you're in. Sometimes it's best just to get out of the way and keep a very low profile in these situations.

Your ability to make executives feel comfortable enough to perform credibly can be a major selling point in your hunt for future employment.

In a noninterview acting situation, executives are generally very nervous and very stiff. So are regular employees, like the secretary on loan who has to say a line. In these cases it's up to you to do a little educating in a very relaxed manner. You'll need to instruct the nonprofessional "actor" about the "hurry up and wait" nature of the videotaping process and, again, offer steady reassurance.

## Your Expectations of Them

Producers and directors have many expectations of you, but should you expect anything from them? Of course you should! However, in the industrial video environment you must be reasonable.

You should expect to be treated as a professional but not a star. You should receive periodic breaks and be told how long they are. Lunch should be a decent, hot meal. You should always be treated courteously. And you should be given privacy to change and make up. Sound pretty basic?

Sometimes what should be done doesn't get done in the industrial video environment, and you'll just have to adapt if you want to be asked back. The worst thing you can do is react negatively when things aren't up to par.

One of the ways to ensure that your working conditions will be as good as they can be is to discuss everything up front. At the time of booking you have a right to know what you will be paid, including overtime if it's not a union shoot.

I once made the classic error of not asking the producer about overtime in advance and paid for it dearly on the job. After fourteen hours of shooting every day for three days, I was informed that there was no overtime being paid for the shoot. Needless to say I vented my anger at this information, alienated the producer and director, and left the job under a cloud. In retrospect, I could have handled the situation in a more professional manner.

Ask about money up front. Ask how the day will progress. Will you need to memorize? Will the script be teleprompted? Will you be permitted to use an earprompter?

When producers call and ask if you are available on a certain date and you say yes, follow that up with "What did you have in mind?" Feel them out and get them to be as specific as you can so that you not only know what's going on but also have the opportunity to beg off gracefully if you don't like what you hear.

When it comes to rates, unless it's a union job, be prepared to negotiate. You may want to negotiate higher than "scale" union rates, too, if you can justify working above the scale. Don't give your services away, but don't be inflexible either. Often, price will decide who's hired. But there's a caveat here. If you work cheap—too cheap—people may begin to think you're not worth very much.

It's fair to expect that the shoot will run according to a preplanned production schedule and that you will be paid overtime even if it isn't a union situation. You should always expect overtime when it occurs, but it's wise to throw in the first hour if you can for obvious public relations reasons. When unforeseen things go wrong, it's often not the fault of the producer/director. Your willingness to give them a break on overtime will increase the likelihood of your being re-hired.

Asking money questions at the time of booking is important, and so is requesting a copy of the script. You have a right to get a copy of the script in advance if it's available, particularly if they want it memorized.

Some producers think it's easy for actors to memorize copy on the spot and expect them to do so. But we know better. Demand a script. If they refuse to send you one, it might be one of those jobs better turned down unless the refusal is clearly for confidentiality reasons.

Some scripts, particularly Department of Defense scripts, do contain sensitive material, and you won't be able to get a look at them in advance. When this is the case, you'll have to wait until you arrive at the shoot to prepare.

When you arrive at the studio or location, take the director aside and ask about breaks and food and where your place of privacy will be. This is also the time to inform the director of any special needs that you may have—for example, calls you have to place or medicine you need to take.

There will be shoots in which the working conditions will be next to impossible. I once did a video in subzero wind chill on board a destroyer, working with a crew of only two people. I was cast as an on-camera narrator here, and the script was long. There were no bathrooms, no portable heaters, no hot coffee, and no food. Shipbuilders were scurrying about interrupting take after take, and more audio problems occurred than you can possibly imagine. But there *was* a plus side. The people with whom I worked treated me very professionally on a personal level, and I was getting paid. Did I complain about the conditions? Only humorously, but so did everyone else.

Which brings this discussion to a very important point. When things go wrong, no matter whose fault a problem is—yours, the crew's, the director's—it will always work to your advantage if you react with a sense of humor. People like to work with likeable people, don't they?

## Working in the Audio Booth

Expect things to operate a little differently when you've been hired for a voice-over. Usually you'll work with only a director and an audio engineer, but sometimes a client or two will show up. In the close quarters of an audio studio, clients tend to give much more direction to talent than they do in television studios or on location. But you should remember that it's the director you really need to please.

What usually happens when a client is around is that the director, who has to be diplomatic in this situation, will have you read the copy to the satisfaction of the client. You may then be asked to read the copy with alterations to satisfy the director. In any case, expect plenty of interpretive variations in the audio booth, as well as close direction.

Audio directors can get very picky and you mustn't let it faze you. You are expected to take direction in a spirit of co-operation. In the final analysis, the director will try to help you achieve a technically perfect and involved reading.

To meet these goals, you need to believe in what you are reading and commit to the script. The director knows that your target listener will not respond properly to the copy if you are not believable.

I recommend your asking for the script in advance of the session so you can prepare. But most often you will not see the copy until you arrive at the studio. When this happens, ask for time to read through the script to get a sense of it to help your interpretation and cut down on the number of mistakes you'll make during the session.

And you will make mistakes. Count on it. But don't allow yourself to get flustered when this occurs. Directors *expect* voice talent to make mistakes. So when you make one, just pause to allow the audio engineer to make an edit, and continue—unless the director wants you to stop and begin again at another point in the script.

Approach all audio work in as relaxed a frame of mind as you can. Get plenty of rest the night before the session, and make sure you eat a couple of hours before you begin recording—you don't want your stomach to growl!

Wear "quiet," comfortable clothes to the session. Cotton and wool blends are fine, but avoid fabrics that rustle when you move. Studio microphones pick up even the slightest sounds.

Bring a pencil to the session so you can mark up the copy to remind you what needs to be emphasized, sped up, slowed down, and so on as dictated by the director.

In truth there is no great mystery to what happens in an audio booth. You go in, say hello, prepare yourself, and get down to the business of reading. The first few times you'll probably have to fight off some nervousness, but after a while you'll get used to the environment and learn what works best for you.

Remember: In voice work, efficiency really matters. Here you are being paid by the hour, so the fewer mistakes you make the better. Can you guess what I'm going to say now? Practice reading aloud every day!

# Afterword: It's a Business

> I think of my acting career as a business that needs constant nurturing and reinvestment. Sure, that costs money, but it's also tax deductible.
>
> — *Minor Rootes*
> *Actor*

$B$y now you should have a clear understanding of what it takes to succeed as an actor in the world of industrials. You've learned how to approach this marketplace as a businessperson who acts rather than as an actor who wants to act for business. And part of being a businessperson is giving considerable thought to your future income, not to mention keeping as much of what you earn as possible. Therefore, I'll briefly discuss the concepts of reinvestment, taxes, and continuing education.

## ✳ Reinvestment

Reinvestment means pouring money earned back into the business to generate more business. Successful companies do it all the time. So should you.

As your business acting career begins to gather momentum, plan on reinvesting a substantial percentage of your take-home pay on making contact with new producers, doing follow-ups after jobs performed, and improving your personal business image and wardrobe.

First, invest in custom promotional materials as discussed in chapter 5 and begin sending them out regularly.

Initially, you'll want to do regular mailings to lots of producers, which means headsheets, audio and video demo tapes, postcards, and December holiday cards. Obviously, this will cost money. But in the long run it will pay off, because as you land jobs you'll also—hopefully—be added to the stock companies of several producers. Then you can slow down your marketing efforts accordingly and begin to invest in even more expensive business aids.

If and when you reach the point where you are a corps member of a dozen or more producers, you'll work regularly and can turn down work due to conflicts. This level is a touchy place to be; on the one hand, you want to work every day and be known as an actor who is in demand but, on the other hand, you don't want to be perceived as too difficult to book. Therefore, if—and it's a big if—you do arrive at this lofty position, you will have to limit mailings to new producers until you work your way out of a corps or two, which will happen.

After a while producers either tire of their corps members or feel that they have become overexposed within the corporation. These attitudes are human nature as well as the nature of business. As you find yourself removed from a corps you will most definitely want to be added to a new one, which is an ideal time to do another batch of mailings.

You also should get in the habit of doing less expensive, selective mailings to follow up on jobs and interviews to simply thank individuals.

How many mailings should you do in all? Most successful business actors will tell you that they send out hundreds of pieces of mail yearly at substantial cost. But they get it all back, of course, and much much more.

As soon as you can afford it, begin rounding out your wardrobe to go beyond the basics discussed earlier. Your image as a successful professional business actor will be enhanced if you show up on jobs with lots of quality wardrobe alternatives. For example, I now have eleven camera-ready business suits, eight sport coats, thirty or so ties, and several business shirts hanging in my business closet at all times. When I started out I had one gray suit and a camel blazer.

And yes, I do have a business closet. I also have a room in my home where I study for work, prepare my mailings, and do recordkeeping. I suggest you do the same. And if you have children—I have six—insist that your business space be off limits. You will need the security of knowing that all of your business materials, including wardrobe and make-up, will remain in perfect condition even while you are away. Lock your closet if you must. Lock you office, too, if that's what it takes. You just won't be able to afford returning home after a business trip to find that one of the kids has worn to a banquet the outfit you need tomorrow.

Reinvestment also applies to tools such as earprompters. It makes sense, if you have the money, to go for the best right away. But if your resources are limited start out with the best you can afford and plan to upgrade as soon as is practical. Using the earprompter as an example, you could purchase a manual unit at about a one-third of the cost to start and go for a wireless later.

The whole point behind reinvestment is that you will be spending money to make more money. And while you're doing that you may find that you're saving money, because of tax deductibility.

## ✳ Taxes

I'm no accountant and I'm not going to tell you how to do your taxes. But if your circumstances allow, you may find that almost every dollar you spend on your business of acting will be allowed as income deductions by the Internal Revenue Service if you qualify as self-employed.

As you embark on your acting career, whether it's comprehensive or limited to the corporate arena, check with a good accountant who is experienced with the tax liabilities of performing artists on how you should approach your taxes. To discover who these accountants are, ask around. If you've read this volume, you know where.

I also recommend that you read Carla Messman's excellent book, *The Artist's Tax Guide & Financial Planner*,[1] for a comprehensive look at artists and taxes. You will learn from this book to keep records of *everything*.

## ✳ Continuing Education

Finally, a word about continuing education. Most of the successful actors I know never stop learning about their craft. Very few figure they've learned all there is to learn. Reinvest some of those hard-earned dollars into developmental courses to improve your performance.

For business actors, I'd recommend courses in television direction, television lighting and audio, television production, and—perhaps most strongly—video and film editing. All of these courses could be taken in addition to the acting courses recommended earlier and would add greatly to your knowledge and understanding of what's going on around you.

So that's it. *Acting in Industrials: The Business of Acting for Business.* Now that you've read it, it's time for you to put it to practice.

Good luck!

------

1. Published by Lyons & Burford, 31 W. 21st Street, New York, NY 10010.